*Dany Laferrière*
translated by *David Homel*

# THE **WORLD** IS
# **MOVING**
# **AROUND** ME

*A Memoir of the Haiti Earthquake*

ARSENAL PULP PRESS  VANCOUVER

Originally published as *Tout bouge autour de moi*
Copyright © 2011 by Éditions Grasset et Fasquelle

THE WORLD IS MOVING AROUND ME
by Dany Laferrière
Translation copyright © 2013 by David Homel
Foreword copyright © 2013 by Michaëlle Jean

ARSENAL PULP PRESS
Suite 101 – 211 East Georgia St.
Vancouver, BC V6A 1Z6
Canada
*arsenalpulp.com*

The publisher gratefully acknowledges the support of the Canada Council for the Arts and the British Columbia Arts Council for its publishing program, and the Government of Canada (through the Canada Book Fund) and the Government of British Columbia (through the Book Publishing Tax Credit Program) for its publishing activities.

The publisher gratefully acknowledges the financial support of the Government of Canada through the National Translation Program for Book Publishing for its publishing activities.

This translation, including the section "How It Came to Be," is based on the Quebec edition published in 2010 by Mémoire d'encrier.

The quotation from Amos Oz, *The Same Sea*, was translated by Nicholas de Lange.

Publisher's note: During the course of the translation, the writer used his authorial privilege to make certain changes to his original text.

Cover photograph by Getty Images
Book design by Gerilee McBride
Editing by Susan Safyan

Printed and bound in Canada

Library and Archives Canada Cataloguing in Publication:

Laferrière, Dany
    The world is moving around me : a memoir of the Haiti earthquake / Dany Laferrière ; translated by David Homel.

Translation of: Tout bouge autour de moi.
Issued also in electronic format.
ISBN 978-1-55152-498-6

    1. Haiti Earthquake, Haiti, 2010. 2. Laferrière, Dany.
I. Title.

QE535.2.H34L3313 2013    551.22097294    C2012-906803-9

FSC
www.fsc.org
MIX
Paper from
responsible sources
FSC® C103214

*For the little group at the Hôtel Karibe*
*who faced the wrath of the gods with me:*
*Michel Le Bris, Maëtte Chantrel, Mélani Le Bris,*
*Isabelle Paris, Agathe du Bouäys,*
*Rodney Saint-Éloi, and Thomas Spear*

In the face of death
There should be neither joy nor sadness
Just a long astonished gaze

—*Renaud Longchamps*

*Foreword*

# The Right Honourable Michaëlle Jean
*Special Envoy for Haiti for the United Nations Educational, Scientific and Cultural Organization and former Governor General of Canada*

The "Étonnants voyageurs" international festival of books and film was about to take place in Haiti in January 2010 when, suddenly, all hell broke loose. The deadliest earthquake in the country's history threw the nation into shock and horror.

Dany Laferrière was among the novelists, poets, and publishers staying at the Hôtel Karibe, overlooking the city of Port-au-Prince.

Not only did the ground beneath their feet betray them, as the earth let loose a deafening growl, but words failed them when it came time to describe that moment of truth, when brutal reality left the voice of fiction speechless.

The only solid things that remained in their lives were those everyday actions that helped them hold onto what had collapsed: the few landmarks still standing amid an inferno of rubble; the few loved ones left among the survivors, who were themselves damaged, riddled with cracks.

Dany Laferrière, faithful guardian and watchman, would work to recover his senses and his stability in the face of this catastrophe and try to make meaning of it.

One day he wrote, "No one can tell a story exactly as it happened. We piece it together. We try to find the essential emotions. In the end, we fall into nostalgia. And if there's one thing that's far from truth, it's nostalgia. So that's not your story."

I read *The World Is Moving around Me* with this premise in mind—that this is a story that's not his to tell. In the way he follows the stream of events, and renders impressions, images, scenes, and conversations in the midst of tragedy or on its periphery, on the path of nostalgia for places that have been destroyed, for those people who have vanished, for memories wounded and devastated, we feel his restraint, something akin to prudishness. There are no special effects. Nothing literary.

And yet, when a journalist asks him—as a man of letters who has witnessed all of this—what the value of culture is, when faced with such suffering, he answers, "When everything else collapses, culture remains." In Haiti, nothing is truer. Witnesses will say, and Laferrière will confirm it, that after the initial shock and for the nights that followed, as the tremors continued to punish the city, people joined together to sing as a way of fighting their misfortune. He reminds us of the lesson and the imagery of Haiti's naïve painters, who choose to portray nature at its most generous, a Garden of Eden, a paradise lost, while all around them, desolation reigns.

The original French-language edition of this book is published in Quebec by Mémoire d'encrier, Rodney Saint-Éloi's company. Dany and Rodney were sitting at a table at a hotel restaurant in Port-au-Prince when "the earth started shaking like a sheet of paper whipped by the wind." This book is filled with a sense of fraternity, informed by the love of a country that never deserts its sons and daughters who live far from it. And I'm one of them.

*Life Returns*

Life seems to have gotten back to normal after decades of trouble. Laughing girls stroll through the streets late into the evening. Painters of naïve canvases chat with women selling mangos and avocados on dusty street corners. Crime seems to have retreated. In lower-class neighborhoods like Bel-Air, criminals aren't tolerated by a population exasperated by everything it has gone through over the last fifty years: family dictatorships, military coups, repeated hurricanes, devastating floods, and random kidnappings. I've come for a literary festival that will bring together writers from around the world to Port-au-Prince. It is an exciting occasion: for the first time, literature seems to have supplanted politics in the public mind. Writers are on television more often than elected officials, which is rare in a country with such a political temperament. Literature is recovering its rightful place. Back in 1929, in his lively book *Hiver caraïbe*, Paul Morand noted that in Haiti, everything ends with a collection of poems. Later, Malraux, after his last journey to Port-au-Prince in 1975, spoke of a nation of painters. People are still looking for the reason behind the high concentration of artists in such a small space. Here in Haiti, a country that occupies just a third of the island it shares with the Dominican Republic, in the Caribbean Sea.

*The Minute*

I was in the restaurant at the Hôtel Karibe with my friend Rodney Saint-Éloi, the publisher at Mémoire d'encrier, who had just come in from Montreal. Under the table, two overloaded suitcases filled with his latest titles. I was waiting for my lobster (*langouste*, on the menu) and Saint-Éloi for his fish in sea salt. I was biting into a piece of bread when I heard a terrible explosion. At first I thought it was a machine gun (others will say a train) right behind me. When I saw the cooks dashing out of the kitchen, I thought a boiler had exploded. It lasted less than a minute. We had between eight and ten seconds to make a decision. Leave the place or stay. Very rare were those who got a good start. Even the quickest wasted three or four precious seconds before they understood what was happening. Thomas Spear, the critic, another of the friends I was with, wasted three precious seconds finishing his beer. We don't all react the same way. And no one knows where death will be waiting. The three of us ended up flat on the ground in the middle of the courtyard, under the trees. The earth started shaking like a sheet of paper whipped by the wind. The low roar of buildings falling to their knees. They didn't explode; they imploded, trapping people inside their bellies. Suddenly we saw a cloud of dust rising into the afternoon sky. As if a professional dynamiter had received the express order to destroy an entire city without blocking the streets so the cranes could pass.

*Silence*

When I travel, I always keep two things with me: my passport (in a pouch around my neck) and a black notebook in which I write down everything that crosses my field of vision or my mind. While I was lying on the ground, I thought of those disaster movies and wondered if the earth would gape open and swallow us up. That was my childhood terror. We found refuge on the hotel tennis courts. I expected to hear screams and cries. There was none of that. In Haiti, they say that as long as no one has screamed, death isn't real. Someone shouted that it was dangerous to stay under the trees. That turned out not to be true. Not a single branch or flower moved during the forty-three seismic disturbances of that first night. I can still hear the silence.

## Projectiles

A 7.3 magnitude earthquake is not so bad. You still have a chance. Concrete was the killer. The population had joined in an orgy of concrete over the last fifty years. Little fortresses. The wood and sheet-metal houses, more flexible, stood the test. In narrow hotel rooms, the TV set was the enemy. People sit facing it. It came right down on them. Many got hit in the head.

## The Ladder

We slowly got to our feet like zombies in a B-movie. I heard cries from the courtyard. The buildings at the rear and to the right had collapsed. These were apartments rented by the year to foreign families, most of them French. Two teenage girls were in a panic on their second-floor balcony. Very quickly, people looked for a way to help them. Three men took up position at the foot of the building. Two were holding a ladder. The young man who'd had the intelligence to go looking for the ladder climbed to the top. The older girl managed to step over the balcony railing. She made it to the ground. Everyone gathered to help her. The young man climbed up the ladder again to bring down the younger girl, who refused to leave the building. She insisted on waiting for her mother. No one knew there was a third person up there. The rescuers worked silently, sweating. They had to act fast because the building, on its last legs, could come down at the slightest vibration. The teenage girl screamed that her mother was inside. She had tried to escape down the stairs and had gotten trapped. The girl was crying and pointing to the spot where her mother had disappeared. From the garden, we watched the girl who believed that if she came down, we'd forget all about her mother. Everyone was working feverishly since the earth had trembled again. The mother managed to free herself by breaking a window. She rushed to her daughter who still refused to climb down until she did. Only when her mother was on solid ground did she accept the ladder.

## The Hotel Employees

Impeccable in their uniforms, the hotel employees never lost their composure. There was a little panic at the beginning, but mostly from the guests who were running in every direction. Some had to be rescued from their rooms because they refused to come out. They were found walking in circles or sitting on their beds with stunned expressions. I watched the staff do everything possible to provide a decent level of service. Maybe the fact they had a function to fulfill helped them walk straight, while the guests went staggering past. As soon as someone was hungry, they would arrive single file with platters of hors d'oeuvres that they lined up on a broad table. They were preparing a reception in the big meeting room by the restaurant. The food was ready. Now we could enjoy it. Near the low gate that led to the tennis courts where we had taken shelter, the security guards stood. They did their best to reassure the customers. I say customers rather than tourists, since the latter are rare in Haiti. Instead, you find members of the many NGOs that have sprouted up over the last decades, sun-tanned journalists who haven't gotten around to leaving the island and foreign businessmen talking in low voices over breakfast with Haitian politicians bathed in sweat. In the garden, the hotel owner went by, inspecting the damage. Walking slowly, his face care-worn, he seemed lost in thought. I'd have given anything to know what was going through his mind. The damage was not just material. In less than a minute, some saw their lifelong dreams go up in smoke. That cloud in the sky a while back was the dust of their dreams.

*The Bathroom*

I imagine the fear of people who were in the bathroom when the earthquake struck. Everyone was caught off guard, but those who were in the shower must have experienced pure panic. You always feel more vulnerable naked, especially covered in soapy water. A lot of people, in their hurry to get out, left the water running.

*Objects*

The enemy isn't time, but all those things we've accumulated with the passage of time. Once we start collecting, we can't stop. Every object demands another. That's the portrait of a life. They'll find bodies by the door. A suitcase next to them.

## Where Are You, Honey?

It's very rare for all the members of one family to be together in the same place, at the same time, in a big city. Especially at 4:53 in the afternoon. People have left work, but they haven't gotten home. No one can be completely sure where the others are. In a family that's trying to make ends meet, if the mother is in one place, the father is somewhere else. Never both in the same spot. The children hang out after school. Only the grandparents are at home. All around me, people were shouting into their cell phones. "Where's your brother? Where's your sister? Mama, answer me, please! Where are you, honey? Have you talked to the kids? Where should we meet?" The conversations ended with the shouted observation, as if the other party could hear, "The line's gone out!" They tried to borrow someone else's phone. The problem was widespread. They paced, feverishly pushing buttons on the slender object that could put them in touch with someone close to them. Picture an entire city where everyone is trying to find a family member or a friend. They shout louder and louder into their phones. They hear the other person less and less. They lose patience. People are concentrated on their personal dramas. Language is whittled down to the essential. Then comes silence.

## *Night*

Most residents of Port-au-Prince spent the first night outside. The previous nights had been chilly. This one was warm and star-lit. I hadn't slept outside since childhood. Lying on the ground, we felt each of the earth's convulsions in our very being. Our bodies were one with the ground. I was pissing against a tree when my legs started trembling: the impression that the earth was shaking. I walked through the garden, amazed to see that the most fragile flowers were still hanging from their stems. The earthquake attacked what was hard, solid, what could resist it. The concrete fell. The flowers survived.

*Time*

I never knew sixty seconds could last so long. And that a night could be endless. No radio: the antennae have fallen. No TV either. No Internet. The cell phone network is gone—though we had time for a few quick calls to the people who matter most to us. A strange moment when we realize we've lost the ability to contact people far away from here. All those wires that link us are cut. We can communicate with those immediately around us, who can hear our voices, but no one else. Human time is now contained in the sixty seconds that the first violent tremors took to change our lives.

*Place*

When it happened, people were scattered here and there: at home (the grandparents and the sick), at school (those slow to leave because class ended an hour earlier), at work (the best employees are often the last to clock out), in the supermarkets (those who have steady pay), in the outdoor markets (no danger for anyone there), in the streets (more than half of the population).

An enormous number of people were caught in the monstrous traffic jams that paralyze Port-au-Prince during rush hour. The uproar suddenly stopped at 4:53 in the afternoon. The fateful hour that cut Haitian time in two. We gaze at Port-au-Prince with the stunned air of a child whose toy has just been accidentally stepped on by an adult.

*The Radio*

A car parked by the sidewalk, its motor still running. The radio was playing. People have stopped bothering to cut the engine when they leave their cars. I was trying to get news of other parts of the city. People wanted to know how bad the damage was. But I heard only static, or a pre-recorded program. I turned the dial and tuned in RFI (Radio France Internationale) that gave no news of the earthquake, at least not yet. I turned off the radio. Where was the driver? People were figuring it was less dangerous on foot. They left their cars behind and took to the road, often with no destination. People who had never done more than a hundred meters on foot walked kilometers that night and felt no fatigue. Their minds were so upset, they lost all awareness of their bodies. Two groups of people who seldom rub shoulders in this city: those on foot and those who own a car. Two parallel worlds that meet only by accident. "You can't know your neighbor if you drive through the neighborhood," said a grieving mother who lost her son. She said that the poorest residents—whom she had never met before, even though she passed through the area twice a day—were the first to support her when she learned that her son was dead in the wreckage of his house. For once, in this city ruled by social barriers, everyone moved at the same speed.

*A Prayer*

Night falls suddenly as it always does in the tropics. We whisper our fears to each other. Now and then, we hear a muffled cry: someone has managed to reach a family member on the phone and has gotten news. A young bank clerk tells me he is afraid to call home for fear of what he might find out. His family lives in Pacot, one of the hardest hit zones. I don't know what to say. Suddenly, a man gets to his feet and begins telling us that the earthquake is the result of our unspeakable behavior. His voice rises in the night. We quiet him down because he's waking the children who have just fallen asleep. A lady tells him to pray in his heart. He walks away, insisting that you can't ask the Lord's forgiveness in a low voice. A group of girls launches into a religious song, so soft that some adults manage to fall asleep. Two hours later, the air is full of noise. Hundreds of people are praying and singing in the streets. For them, this is the end of the world announced by Jehovah. Next to me, a little girl wants to know if there will be school tomorrow. A breath of childhood settles over us all.

*Animals*

Dogs and roosters kept us company through the night. The Port-au-Prince rooster crows whenever he feels like it. Normally I hate this habit. But that night, I listened for his cry. We didn't hear cats meowing. Port-au-Prince is more a dog city. Dogs, most often in the streets, survived, while the cats that hid under beds and in closets didn't make it. As for the birds, they took flight at the first movement of the earth.

## The Crowd

On that first night, the city was filled with a disciplined, generous, and restrained crowd. People ceaselessly moving with oth-
er-worldly determination. They seemed unconcerned with the
pain they bore with an elegance admired the world over. The rest
of the planet was glued to the small screen, watching the strange
ceremony wherein the living and the dead mingled so perfectly
they couldn't be told apart. Malraux, just before his death, traveled to Haiti because he felt that the painters of Saint-Soleil had
intuitively discovered something that makes all struggle against
death fruitless. A secret path. People were amazed by that ability to remain in the wreckage so long without eating or drinking.
That's because they're used to eating very little. How can they take
to the road and leave everything behind? They have so little in the
first place. The fewer objects we possess, the freer we are—and
I'm not singing the praises of poverty. Haiti's misfortune was not
what moved the world: it was the way the Haitian people stood
up to misfortune. We gazed with wonder as the disaster revealed
a nation whose rotten institutions prevent it from coming into its
own. When those institutions disappeared from the landscape,
even for a moment, we discovered a proud yet modest people
through the clouds of dust.

*A Song*

The children have been sleeping for a while. Shadows pass in the garden. Security staff keeping an eye out. Suddenly a song rises. We hear it in the distance. A guard tells us that outside (we're quite far from the road) is a large crowd of people singing. Their voices are harmonious. That's when I understood that everyone was affected. And that something of unimaginable depth had occurred. People were in the streets. They sang to calm their pain. A forest of human beings moving slowly across the still trembling ground. I saw shadows descending the mountains to join them. How do they manage to dissolve so quickly in the crowd? The song they were singing to the heavens, in the whitish light of breaking dawn, united them.

*Forty-Three Tremors*

From time to time, a slight tremor awakens our fears. The earth is shuddering as if it could not find its rest. People say it's not over. That other major shocks await us. All that is just rumors since the seismologists have yet to speak. But we can't seek stable shelter yet, because what if things degenerate again? So we wait. With each new tremor, as small as it may be, people who were drifting off lift their heads like startled lizards. I hear muffled cries. No one knows what the next few seconds have in store. We don't know what is stirring beneath our bellies. You can hide from the wind or even from fire, but not from the earth that moves beneath your feet. We glance at each other to gauge our neighbor's fear and measure our own. By the fence around the tennis courts, next to a dozing security guard, a small radio is spitting out sound. Sometimes we even understand what it's saying. Often a voice is shouting out advertisements for mattresses. Which is ironic when most of the city is sleeping on the ground.

## The Concrete Trap

A lady who lives nearby spent all night talking to her family still trapped beneath a ton of concrete. First her husband stopped responding. Then one of their three children. Later, another. She kept begging them to hold out a little longer. More than a dozen hours later, people were finally able to rescue the baby, who had been crying the whole time. When he got out, he broke into a wide smile.

*The Revolution*

The radio announced that the Presidential Palace has been destroyed. The taxation and pension office, destroyed. The courthouse, destroyed. Stores, crumbled. The communication network, destroyed. Prisoners on the streets. For one night, the revolution had come.

*The First Messages*

Day breaks. We awake slowly. Some are still sleeping, especially those who stayed up all night. The night is frightening; the day, reassuring. A mistake to believe that, since everything happened in broad daylight. We're still in the hotel garden, under the spreading trees, elated to be among the living, even if we lack the essentials. We try to reach our friends. The means of communication (cell phones, land lines, Internet) are still not working up to capacity. Someone shouts that there is Internet access in front of the hotel. We rush over there. I'm amazed by this group ability to find a solution when everything seems blocked. We fan out, then someone shouts, "It's here!" I go running and discover a row of people sitting on the ground at the entrance to the hotel, feverishly sending messages to their loved ones. We need to act fast because the connection, we're told, can go down at any minute. A guy next to me, his face running with sweat, is staring at his screen. I see he's looking at the news. I grab the machine from him. He turns to me, incredulous, but doesn't try to take it back. I send my first message to my wife: "I'm all right but the city is broken." I add that Saint-Éloi is all right too and that we're together every second, day and night. Our little group has washed up on a desert island the day after a ferocious storm.

*The Outside World*

We were sitting around a table talking in the hotel garden when Lyonel Trouillot the writer showed up. He told us what happened the day before, once night fell. Everything was pitch dark, but he left his house and headed for the hotel. Trouillot walked the entire way last night, to the hotel and back, two hours in total darkness. Knowing his health problems, the effort must have been superhuman. Today, he seemed relaxed. He had his car now. I decided to use the opportunity to go see my mother, since I haven't been able to reach her by phone. Saint-Éloi will join us. The hotel is set back from the main road by a hundred meters or so, just enough to separate us from the city. We leave the hotel life and fall into the cauldron of Port-au-Prince and its suffocating reality.

### The Mango Lady

She's the first thing I see on the road to Pétionville. A mango vendor sitting with her back against a wall, a dozen mangos spread out before her. This is her livelihood. For her, there's nothing new. It doesn't occur to me to buy from her, though I love mangos. I hear Saint-Éloi's voice behind me: "What a country!" These people are so used to finding life in difficult conditions that they could bring hope down to hell.

*The First Bodies*

Just outside Pétionville, I see bodies on the ground. Carefully stacked one next to the other, eight in all. I don't know how they died or who put them here. The houses are below. Modest structures made of sheet metal. We wonder who could have placed the bodies by the side of the road. Not the government; it hasn't recovered its wits. Not the families either, who would have found a way to bury them. Maybe the dead were just passing through, anonymous here. People are always on the move in a city where it's hard to find a job. They look for life wherever it can be found. Later I learn that the dead are so numerous they can't be buried individually. The figure climbs by the hour and takes over everything, to the point that people don't talk about the dead, but only their number.

*Rhythm*

We reach Pétionville. I spot a dozen broken houses. Maybe there are more. I can see only those along the road. Pétionville itself seems to have survived. I breathe a little easier. People are standing in small groups on the sidewalk, talking. I expected crowds crushed by pain, but daily life has already resumed its rhythm. Even misfortune can't slow down the incessant activity in one of the poorest regions of the world.

*A Bon Vivant*

A man is standing by a big red gate. "That's my father," Saint-Éloi says. The same warm spark in his eyes. And the same way of thrusting out his chest. The two look too much alike not to be fellow pleasure-seekers. Saint-Éloi described his father as a bon vivant who likes cooking and chatting up the young vendors who pass by his door. A man whose interest in women has never slackened. Saint-Éloi gets out of the Jeep and goes to see him. I stay in the car. They talk for a while, touching each other on the forearm from time to time. Ten minutes later he returns. His father waves to us and closes the gate. "Everything all right?" I ask Saint-Éloi. "Except for a cousin who was at the Caribbean Market. They say she'd made it to the door when a cement block hit her in the head ... Another step and she would have been safe." We drove in silence to Delmas.

## The Caribbean Market

We enter the enormous district of Delmas, that insatiable monster whose tentacles are getting ready to swallow up Pétionville, the fragile, middle-class suburb where there are more and more poor people. The traffic is intense in Delmas: humans and cars play bull and matador. All kinds of noises (horns, shouting, sirens) rise from a crowd that's always on the edge of explosion. The commercial buildings that line the main road hide thousands of houses of all sizes built in such an anarchic fashion that the place is like a world unto itself. Whoever ventures into this labyrinth for the first time will wander in circles forever unless he finds a helpful soul to show him the way. The government tried unsuccessfully to make the place more orderly by putting numbers on the different entrances. The area looks like it's been bombed. One building in five has collapsed. There are hardly any cars, which makes it amazingly easy to get around. Someone points out the Caribbean Market, always crowded with customers this time of day. My heart tightens at the thought of them under that heap of stones. People blessed with a decent salary would stop to pick up provisions here when they got out of work. They would exchange the latest gossip and use chance meetings to extend invitations of all kinds. The Caribbean Market was the crossroads of the striving middle class that had sprung up in this neighborhood over the last twenty years.

## Money

I noted that very brief moment when money disappeared from circulation. For several hours, in a metropolis of three million people, no one produced a bank note to buy something. With the stores destroyed, merchandise was for the taking. It could only be given away or bartered. Commerce is generally carried out among the living. But, for once, the living were thinking only of the dead and of those who had disappeared, for whom they were searching throughout the city. The moment was brief indeed. People hadn't even buried their dead, and already their thoughts were returning to money. They started thinking about it as soon as the future became imaginable.

## A Yellow Square

That feeling of déjà vu. I know this part of town. Seeing I was upset, Trouillot slowed down. I was right, he told me, that's the Télé-Ginen building. Compè Filo works there. And I was there yesterday at 3:30 in the afternoon. I could have been there at 4:35 too. Between two concrete slabs, I spotted a small yellow square the size of a licence plate. It's all that's left of the little car that took me back to the Hôtel Karibe after my interview with Filo. I combed through the totally flattened building and discovered, at the back, a few photos miraculously spared next to the trophies I'd noticed yesterday on the desk of the Télé-Ginen owner, an affable woman whom Filo was quick to introduce me to. I'd been in a hurry yesterday. I had to be back at the Hôtel Karibe by five o'clock. After a lot of back and forth, since he wanted to drive me himself so we'd have time to talk in the car, Filo finally agreed to let a young journalist drop me off in that little yellow car that was now completely flattened in the wreckage of the building. The place was a strange labyrinth; first I'd come across a chorale of girls dressed in white in a trance, and then I'd listened to a pastor shouting into a screechy microphone. Walking the corridors, I realized they were taping a religious program. Meanwhile, in his studio, Filo was singing the praises of voodoo and popular culture. The building reminded me of a murderous jungle where everything proliferates wildly the minute you turn your back. Now there was no one here, no employee who could tell me what happened to the staff. Everyone seemed preoccupied by his own troubles. I remember thinking as I left Télé-Ginen yesterday that there'd be no survivors if ever fire broke out.

## Musical Chairs

People move through the streets, hoping to come across a family member, a friend, a neighbor, or even an acquaintance: someone to legitimize our claim to be among the living. We're zombies until someone calls our name. The person no one has seen could well be dead. Meanwhile, that other person thinks you're dead, though he hopes to see you alive. There's no way of knowing where death was waiting when you were at that particular place. Some people did all they could to show up at the meeting. Others walked away from the fatal spot a few seconds before. And to think we had no idea we were playing heads or tails with our lives. I left Télé-Ginen to get back to the Hôtel Karibe by five p.m.— but it could have been the other way around. A game of musical chairs the entire city was playing. There were a lot more people than chairs when the music started. You had to find an empty chair when it stopped at exactly 4:53 in the afternoon.

## It

We have no idea what to expect in the coming years. People, like houses, can be divided into three categories: the ones who are dead, those who are gravely injured, and those who are deeply damaged inside but don't know it yet. The latter are the most troubling. The body will keep going for a while before it finally falls to pieces. Suddenly. Without warning. Those people have hidden the screams inside them. One day they will implode. Until then, they seem in perfect health. A mixture of bonhomie and high energy. Happy to exist since their brush with death. They've been able to put a distance between themselves and the images that haunt them. Sometimes they talk about it with a joyful glow in their eyes. How do they do it? That's the point—they're not doing it. You can't have experienced it and go your way as if nothing had happened. It'll catch up to you one day. Why do you say "it"? Because "it" doesn't have a name yet.

## The Lost Friend

I met Filo at the end of the 1970s. Was it at the theater school that took over the large rooms at the Lycée des Jeunes Filles after classes were over? Or was it at the Sylvio Cator Stadium where we went to see the finals between the Racing Club and the Black Eagles or Le Violette? Filo has always been in my life. We were part of the little group of starving kids who mixed art and revolution. Radio Haïti-Inter was recruiting new journalists. Filo went to try out. At the beginning, it didn't work; he was too much a rebel to follow the station's strict rules. He had no notion of time. He would get to his show a half-hour late. In the end, his bosses figured it out: they stuck him at the very end of the day's programming. He could show up when he wanted and do what he felt like. His audience was made up of insomniacs, and he helped them get through the night. The very next day, Filo was a star. His mocking irony and sharp eye—he was a young man from a rough neighborhood—attracted all levels of society right from the start. President Jean-Claude "Baby Doc" Duvalier imprisoned then exiled most of the country's influential journalists in November of 1980, muzzling what was called at the time "the independent press." They all returned when Baby Doc went into exile himself in February of 1986. There was dissension within the group of alternative journalists, which meant that some were left on the outside. Filo wandered in the wilderness of Port-au-Prince for a while. When I asked after him, every time I came through town, often no one knew where he was. I was told he was doing odd jobs, an elegant way of saying that he wasn't part of the tribe anymore. The last time I saw him was at the Hôtel Kinam in 2008; he'd come to interview me for his show on Télé-Ginen. Filo was in a class by himself. The others in the group didn't seem to have progressed much, but he'd made changes in his head. Of course he still talked about religion, which scared the Haitian left, but he was as sharp-minded as ever. And subtle enough not to impose his beliefs on other people. That day he gave me a present: an image of the Black Virgin of Poland that believers in voodoo take for the Polish version of the goddess Erzulie. I still have it. With his traditional dress and his peasant hat, Filo looked like he'd never left the 1970s, a time marked by the furious search for authenticity among intellectuals. Despite his choice of clothes, he was one of the liveliest minds in the country. When I came back for this trip, I met up with him at the beginning of the month in front of the Rex Theatre, and we set a date for January 12. I went to the radio station in Delmas. We started the interview more than an hour late. Filo gave the false impression of being interested only in popular culture, whereas he knew plenty about a lot of things. I knew his little mannerisms, like that sideways smile that let you know he was nobody's them any more, or steal or kill or torture or make promises you have no intention of keeping, consoling someone who just lost a loved one, lying on a hospital deathbed, playing soccer, coming to Port-au-Prince for the first time or leaving the country (an airplane has just taken off). All these small acts bind us together and weave the great cloth of humanity. At 4:53 in the afternoon, our memory trembled.


## A Green Jeep

A horn sounds three times. The green Jeep that was following pulls up next to us. What's going on? Arms reach out of the open doors like branches of a leafless tree. They tell us they've been driving around town, saying hello to the living. We turn right. My mother lives at Delmas 31.

## At Frankétienne's Place

We wander in circles through this labyrinth of alleyways; most of them turn into dead ends. Finally, we get onto a street that slopes up toward Frankétienne's place. The massive red wall that made his house look like a small fortress is badly damaged. A twisted electric pole blocks the entrance. Wires hang along the gate. A neighbor tells us he's there. I look up. There's a gaping hole in the wall. His library is devastated. We push open the gate, careful not to touch the wires on the ground. There's no sense getting electrocuted after surviving an earthquake. He hears our voices and comes out. I've never seen him so upset. Red as a boiled lobster. No theatrics this time: he is naked in his pain. He hugs us and won't let go. His wife appears, as discreet as ever, in his shadow. Her smile is sadder than usual. Frankétienne tells us his version of the event. He carries the city inside him. He turns toward his gutted house, overwhelmed. He heard a locomotive noise like most people, then decreed it was "the sound of all that Port-au-Prince contains breaking up." A poet talking. The cloud he first thought was a great fire turned out to be "the dust of my city." The city and his body are one. We avoid looking at each other. The cry of a bird in the noonday sky. Frankétienne watches it fly toward the bare mountains that surround Port-au-Prince, then he takes up his story again. He was on the terrace with a

South American journalist when it happened. Since he's in symbiosis with the elements, he immediately understood it was an earthquake. With the journalist on his heels, he rushed down the stairs, grabbed his wife in the kitchen, and ran into the courtyard. He was out of breath by the end of his story. Though he's often caught in the web of banal details of daily life, finally he had an event equal to his gargantuan appetites. Only one place was spared: the garden where we often met to discuss Tolstoy, Joyce, or God (Franketienne doesn't bother with small fry). We stood a moment in silence, and then Franketienne, as if suddenly remembering we were there, urged us to view the damage. Paintings on the floor. The broad walls covered in frescoes were shattered. His house is an art gallery devoted to his work. His books were scattered everywhere. He's both artist and businessman—a Renaissance man. The last time I visited, he brought me to his little warehouse where he keeps hundreds of paintings. He told me to choose one. I can't bring myself to ask him about the state of his warehouse. And now, with all necessary gestures, he launches into a description of how he was rehearsing a play about the earthquake a half-hour before it struck. Standing in the garden, he begins declaiming. We stand back to give him space for his theater. He speaks of a Port-au-Prince "that is torn, that is crevassed." Franketienne replays the earthquake with his words. His prophetic one-man show. Marie-Andrée keeps watch so he mind to save the food. When she turned around, the house was a heap of stones. She wants to know why she wasn't allowed to die with her family. We wait for her to stop before going on our way.

## At My Mother's

My mother lives close to Frankétienne's. We turn left at the first alleyway. My heart tightens. But the houses on her narrow, shaded street, by some miracle, look untouched. We drive slowly. The silence is unusual. As if the country had frozen. I have absolutely no idea what to expect. My heart leaps when I spot my brother-in-law (Christophe Charles, the poet) by the big red gate. He looks worried, but no more than he usually does. We leave the car by the wall. I see that the new house just across from my mother's is completely destroyed. Nothing can be done. The owner was so proud of it. My brother-in-law's thin smile reassures me. I figure that if something had happened, he wouldn't be standing outside. But I try not to come to any hasty conclusions, because you never know. I shake Christophe's soft hand, and he lets us go by. Everyone is in the yard, even my nephew Dany (we have the same name to keep the dictator, who pushed me into exile, from having the last word). A shiver runs through me when I realize Dany could have been at the university or somewhere else when the earthquake struck. By chance he'd stopped by the house, since he didn't usually get home before nightfall. Delmas 31 is hard to reach (public transit doesn't go there), and he has no car. Normally his father picks him up after class. But this time he was here. If my nephew hadn't been there, my mother, who's more than eighty years old (she won't even tell me her age), and Aunt Renée, who can't get around without help, would have been alone. And here they are, safe and sound, waiting for me. Aunt Renée is lying on a mattress that was thrown into the yard. She seems comfortable there. My mother is very excited. She takes me in her arms and whispers this litany into my ear: "I've seen it all in this country. Military coups, one hurricane after another, floods that wiped everything out, dictators who hand the country down from father to son, and now an earthquake." She's kept a detailed list of the natural disasters that have befallen us over the last two decades. I don't know whether dictatorship should be included among natural disasters. It might be at the root of these misfortunes, or just their logical extension. My mother insists: "I've seen it all." I stare into her wide eyes that have seen it all. That sadness lasts only a moment. My sister is making us bitter tea that is meant to lower our blood pressure. Aunt Renée grips my hand (hers is bonier than last time). The house doesn't seem damaged. My mother takes me by the arm and shows me a little crack in the living room, and a much bigger one in the bathroom. Not too serious, but enough to worry her. But deep down, we are all so shaken that fear will be part of us for a long time. When it comes in such unexpected and massive fashion, death will not easily leave us. It's so enormous that instead of casting us into sadness, I feel something like drunkenness come over me. Even my sister, who's normally so care-worn, suddenly seems lighter. Today's tragedies have erased yesterday's worries. The feeling that we've finally hit bottom and can only go up. And the simple joy of still being alive.

## My Nephew

I stepped into the yard with my nephew. The little shacks on the other side of the ravine had stood up to the earthquake. The old wall collapsed. We sat on the hood of the car.

"I'm going to write something," I said.

"I imagine ..."

"I'm going to write about this."

I still couldn't give it a name.

"I understand," he said to me in a serious voice.

It's like he's matured overnight.

"What are you thinking about?"

A dog moved up the street. What could it live off, now that people are as destitute as it is? It looked thin and agile enough to find something to eat in the ruins.

"May I ask you something, Uncle?"

I sensed it was something serious.

"I'm listening."

"I'd like to write something about this ..."

"Nothing is stopping you."

His head was lowered, but I could tell he hadn't finished.

"What's wrong?"

"I'd like you not to write about it."

The boy certainly knew what he wanted.

"It doesn't work like that, you know." I showed him my black notebook. "As you can see, I've been taking notes non-stop."

"No," he said, laughing. "That's not what I mean. You can write your journal, but not a novel."

Completely taken aback, I listened as he explained in great detail that this is the event of his generation, not mine. Mine was the dictatorship. His is the earthquake. And his sensitivity will speak of it.

"I can't promise you that. No one book takes the place of another."

I gave him my point of view. In any case, that sort of novel isn't up my alley. It would take a kind of power I don't possess. Besides, nature has already written it. A grandiose novel in the classical style that features a time (4:53 in the afternoon), a place (Haiti), and more than two million characters. You'd have to be Tolstoy to take up a challenge like that. I watched his determined expression. Homer believed the gods send us misfortune so we might make poetry of it. Tolstoy, Homer: we picture ourselves like them before we start writing. But what if this young man has what it takes? Just as I was leaving, my mother slipped an envelope into my pocket.

*The Parish*

We had to make a long detour to reach the Delmas highway. I opened the envelope and found a picture of the Virgin inside. On the back, in pencil, in a trembling hand, it was written that this image had been blessed by the priest of Altagrâce, the church my mother has attended since the family moved to Delmas. It's more difficult to adapt to a new church than a new neighborhood. When we were in Carrefour-Feuilles, she went to Saint-Gérard.

She knew the church well, since it was the same one she attended when we lived in Lafleur-Duchêne, though we were a lot closer to Saint-Alexandre. She went to mass at Saint-Gérard for more than thirty years, which helped her get to know her neighbors. People meet at the market or at church. At first, she had all sorts of complaints about Altagrâce—even the priest's accent exasperated her. She didn't like the poor people there; they were too aggressive compared to the Saint-Gérard parishioners. But now she couldn't picture herself anywhere else. You should have heard her heart-felt hallelujah when I told her Altagrâce had been spared. I have no news about Saint-Gérard, but people say that Carrefour-Feuilles is in ruins.

## Trouillot's House

We get to Lyonel Trouillot's neighborhood. A group of people surround the car. They're shouting and waving their arms. Finally I understand that someone is hurt and needs to be taken to the hospital immediately. Trouillot solves the problem by finding another car. The noise fades. We move slowly toward the house, since people keep hanging on to the car doors to give us news of the neighborhood. We sit in the small yard of a modest house. Plants growing everywhere. I breathe easier. A short time later, the oldest of the Trouillot brothers makes an appearance in a chair (he has trouble walking). He is set down next to us so he can be part of the conversation. Smiling as always, because nothing can get him down. Michel-Rolf Trouillot is the author of the first history of Haiti written in Creole: *Ti dife boule sou istoua Ayiti*. I met him in Montreal when he was working on the book. He was teaching in New York at the time. He couldn't believe that there were no works of history in Creole, the language the slaves used to express themselves, the very ones who struggled to turn the colony into a country. For him, that was the whole point. Neither did he see Creole as the language of the heart, unlike French, the language of the mind. Everyone knows Senghor's formulation: "Emotion is black, and reason, Hellenic." Trouillot's view of Haitian history is Marxist. I remember those debates that dominated the 1980s. I can still see him leap to his feet to clarify a point of history and advance his Marxist vision of events. He wasn't always this old sage who is sitting to my left, a peaceful smile on his lips. A shame that his health problems have kept him from continuing his research with the same intensity. We discuss what has happened, while all around us, people are running every which way as if we were in a war zone. Our calm attitude, which is only superficial, is designed to show others who passion for turning young people into readers. Now he is part of the rescue team working on the hotel up ahead. I stayed there at the beginning of December. I can scarcely imagine the disaster. All this effort to save the Montana, while right next to it people are pleading for help. Is it to bury the dead or save lives? I have no idea. A man standing next to the car remarks, without too much bitterness, that there's more here than the Montana. But it's the place where big contracts are negotiated and important political decisions made. The favorite hotel of the international stars who have gotten interested in human misery. Humanitarian organizations send their people to stay there. And since most journalists (especially the ones from TV) have made the place their headquarters for years, you can imagine the enormous coverage the Montana is enjoying. It's true, there are a lot of dead (and a few survivors) in the ruins of the hotel that collapsed in the first few seconds. The crane that was blocking traffic has finally started climbing toward the top of the slope, and we're waved through.

*How Georges Died*

There are cars in the supermarket parking lot. A dozen or so. We pull into a space. Inside, complete chaos. In the liquor section, half the bottles are on the floor. We walk on broken glass through a pond of red wine. The shelves are nearly empty. Saint-Éloi manages to get his hands on a few cans of sardines. We pick up a dozen bottles of water. People are chatting in line. No electricity: the clerk is concentrating on his little pad of paper as he tallies up the bills. Behind me, an overwrought photographer is announcing the death of Georges and Mireille Anglade. I saw them last night at the hotel where they were attending a private reception. Always that mischievous look in Georges' eye. Such warmth in the way he opens his arms to welcome you. Mireille waits patiently for Georges to finish crushing you against his chest by way of embrace. She is more delicate, with more nuances of feeling, but just as warm. A riddle of a smile. As always, Anglade was laughing, and every inch of flesh on his body danced. These last years, he had put all his energy into promoting the *lodyans*, the narrative form nearest, he maintained, to our way of seeing the world. He believed that Haitians are born storytellers who nowadays express themselves through writing. Recently he reread a good amount of our fiction ("from Independence to the present," in his bulimic fashion) and discovered that our best writers are nocturnal storytellers. Our writing has its wellspring in that orality—that "oralature," as he liked to call it. Georges was exaggerating, of course, but with such a good heart. The man had a kind of energy that could sweep you along like a wave. He loved endless discussions at the dinner table with good friends. A geographer who was also a politician, his true passion was literature. An incorrigible dreamer—that's what he was. I can't imagine him without Mireille. They died together.

## The Sad-Eyed Young Man

Standing near the fence by the tennis courts, I see Chantal Guy come up. She's a journalist with the Montreal daily *La Presse*, and Ivanoh Demers, the photographer, is right behind her. They're both alive, and now they're inseparable. When I was lying in the hotel courtyard with everything moving around me, I thought of Chantal Guy. I'd insisted so much that she come here, even though she had her doubts. It's always difficult to convince people to come to Haiti. First they agree, because the country exerts a fascination. An intense exchange of letters follows, then silence. Friends and relations recommend against the trip. They go on

Internet sites that portray an extremely dangerous place. Panic sets in. In the end, the answer is no. With Chantal, I did more than insist: I argued against each of her objections. For me, it was important for this delegation of Quebec writers to be accompanied by a good journalist. Besides, she's a friend. I've been living in Quebec for thirty-four years, I know everyone on the literary scene, I've read most writers working today, and I felt it was time that Quebec writers come and see how Haitians live in their own country. I don't think it's healthy to have a good friend who knows you so well, who has looked into the hidden zones of your life, but who has no sense of the country you come from. You don't get to know a culture by watching TV documentaries. If you want to get a real idea of things, especially for a journalist, you have to be on the ground. Smell the earth, touch the trees, and meet people in their natural environment. I'm not blaming anyone. I was just hoping for a dialogue between writers from Quebec and Haitian writers who represent the two largest French-speaking populations in the Americas. Chantal held out but finally agreed. And now the earthquake. That's why I thought of her at that critical time. Especially when I heard (that night there were so many rumors) that the Hôtel Villa Créole where she was staying was heavily damaged. And now here she comes, making her entrance like a Venus arising from the ashes with Ivanoh Demers on her heels. He looks ill at ease. Port-au-Prince was a revelation for

Chantal. She used to be afraid of her own shadow, but now she's an intrepid warrior ready to face the fury of the elements. As for Demers, the photos he took that day made him the most famous photographer on the planet, at least that week. His pictures were published in papers around the world. And his moving photo of the young man lifting his eyes to us with a mixture of pain and gravitas will remain in our memories. The gentle light of his face conjures up the Flemish masters. Yet the photographer himself was torn between his sudden celebrity and the city in ruins, since one couldn't exist without the other. He shouldn't feel bad. His photo of the young man's gentle expression will last.

*Culture*

Chantal Guy blurts out a question: what do I think of all this? She takes out her notebook. What is the value of culture in the face of disaster? Asking the question in a university classroom doesn't have the same resonance as it does here. I look around: it's easy to evaluate the situation. The conversations are lively. I hear laughter from time to time. People are looking for some way out. Which makes me think that when everything else collapses, culture remains. The people who are still moving will save this city. The crowd's appetite for life makes living possible in these dusty streets. I go back to the lesson of the old naïve painters who choose to show nature in its splendor when all around there is desolation.

## A Man in Mourning

He is smoking on the street corner, near the art vendors who have started displaying their canvases on the walls again in the wind, heat, and dust. Very elegant in his fine black suit. A black hat. Unconcerned by the bustling activity around him. Unmoving, he lights another cigarette. Some people can keep their composure no matter what. I approach him. He offers me a smoke. We talk about this and that, avoiding the subject of the hour. Slowly I learn a little about him, and I understand he is far from being the dandy he appears to be. His mother died at the beginning of last week and he wasn't able to contribute to her funeral. His three sisters (they live in New York) paid all the expenses, even for his black suit. They were supposed to leave the day before yesterday, but they postponed their departure to buy him a barbershop that was for sale not far from here. He's a barber, but he can't seem to keep a job for long. His sisters thought it would be better if he were his own boss. This isn't the first time they've tried to help him out, but it's the first time his situation as a parasite depressed him to the point that he considered suicide last night. He lights another cigarette (I refused his offer) and we get around to the earthquake. He was here when it happened. He went home and discovered his house was completely destroyed and that his sisters were dead in the wreckage. He stares at the glowing coal of his cigarette a little too long. The pain I read in his eyes is so private I realize I'm intruding. I slipped away as he was taking another drag.

## The Room

I decided to return to my room. The façade that overlooks the garden is badly cracked, but the hotel didn't collapse. Debris everywhere; there's no way of saying how bad the damage is. I go up the stairs to the third floor. From there, I can see that the lobby was wrecked. I continue my adventure without knowing what I'll find. So far, so good, but the hotel could cave in at any moment. I reach my room. The door is closed. I take out my electronic key. No chance it will work. The earthquake must have knocked out the electrical system. Besides, they cut the current to prevent fires. I slip the card in the slot. The little green light lights up. I walk inside. The room is intact except for the television set on the floor. I find my suitcase. The computer that someone lent me hasn't moved from the bedside table. My last two mangos are patiently waiting for me next to the computer. I grab everything I can. I picture everyone doing the same thing at this very moment, trying to save things that matter. Things that might appear useless to other people. I'd better not stay too long; just being here is a major provocation. When it brushes past, death leaves us in a frenetic state that pushes us to defy the gods. That explains this irresistible desire to lie down on the bed. I change my mind at the last second, realizing I'm doing something stupid. It might not be over. A new tremor could send the hotel crashing down. I don't even know how long I've been in the room. I've lost all notion of time since yesterday. I understand now that a minute can hold the entire life of a city. A new density for me. Finally I exit the room, leaving the door open, with the feeling the card won't work a second time.

## *The Opportunity*

We were sitting under the trees when someone showed up with a bottle of rum and set it down in the middle of the table. Some people could find alcohol even in hell. He found this bottle in one of the cabinets in the bar. Apparently it's not the last one. The Gold Rush, all over again. It's the only weapon against the anxiety of the coming night. With a haggard eye, I watch the mosquitoes gather around the light, waiting to go on the attack. Their exasperating music hums in my ears. We drink right from the bottle and pass it around. Now is the time to try everything that good manners and hygiene teach us not to do. The warmth of the rum is good. We'd like to do something completely unusual, since this kind of situation won't happen twice. It was more acceptable last night than tonight, and tomorrow it will be too late. We will have recovered our wits completely. And we won't be just the few of us. Right now, everyone in this city is either dead, wounded, or saved by some miracle. Tomorrow, or even tonight, they will start arriving (are they already among us?), and we will lose our sense of collective madness. In any case, it's not over yet. The earth is still shaking. Two or three points higher on the Richter scale and we'll be cast back into a realm without time. I don't understand why we don't try doing something completely off the beaten track of everyday life. Nothing is holding us back. No more prisons, no more cathedral, no more government, no more school—it's the perfect opportunity to try something new. An opportunity that won't knock twice. The revolution is at hand, and here I am, sitting under a tree.


## An Offering to the Gods

We open the cans of sardines. I remember that I'd left bread on the table in the restaurant. Rodney and I go off in search of that bread. It's the first time we've returned to the scene. Nothing has changed. The restaurant, made of wood, is more flexible than concrete. The breadbasket is sitting where we left it. I feel like I'm stealing an offering made to the gods.


## The Second Night

We settle in. Everybody goes back to the spot where they slept the first night. We've claimed our territory. There's movement by the entrance. The guards are coming with mattresses, sheets, and pillows. The pillow is the sign of a higher plateau of refinement. Our heads won't be on the same level as the rest of our bodies. An enormous change compared to last night. A good night's sleep will make us less sensitive to the smaller tremors. We'll need steady nerves. Already we're leaving behind last night's anxiety, when we weren't even sure we'd see the dawn. Now we're more exasperated than worried. We just wish the earth would stop moving. I spot a red dot moving through the garden: a man smoking a cigarette.

*A Pain in the Ass*

People's temperaments are quickly revealed within this small perimeter. All the major traits of our species are represented here. I suppose it's the same in every improvised camp. You can spot them right off: the petty ones, the jealous types, the generous kind, the optimists, the pessimists, the adventurers, the careful ones, the quiet ones, and the pains in the ass. I've got one of the latter in my zone, a woman. She talks endlessly about her own problems. Most people here have family members either dead or injured, but she couldn't care less. She knows that her husband is alive, but she acts like she isn't sure just to be at the center of attention. She complains about everything. In her opinion, Haitians are partly responsible for this disaster. We must have committed some crime; that's why misfortune follows us. And on and on. She's just decided that it's too beautiful a night to sleep. And she's right: the sky is magnificent and the earth still warm from its convulsions. But I'd rather be attacked by hordes of furious mosquitoes than have her muttering behind my back. I set up my mattress a little further on.

*A Teenager*

He showed up this afternoon, found a spot, and settled in without a sound. He was having trouble with his foot. Maëtte, who has a way with stray dogs, took him under her wing. Especially since he'd lost his parents. She treated his wounds and defended him when a guard wanted to put him out. On the first night, we could welcome strangers into our space, because even the thieves were in a state of shock. Sleeping outside is always a risky business. Tourists possess two things that make thieves covetous: money and a valid passport. Besides, our suitcases were piled up along the fence. The men slept like babies. The women kept watch, listening for the slightest disturbance. They lifted their heads the minute a shadow moved through the garden. Often it was just someone looking for a tree to piss against. The women organized a spot near the fence for their basic needs so they wouldn't have to leave the secure zone. Their anxiety became palpable once darkness began to fall. Luckily there were songs and prayers that were like lullabies in the night.

## Morning Conversation

I spent a while watching a grandmother singing with her grandson. They were sleeping on the other side of the net on the tennis courts. It was a whole other neighborhood. The songs brought my childhood rushing back like a salmon swimming up a river. I heard them talking in low tones as, under the sheet, I noted down the morning thoughts that washed over me in streams. Reveries that had nothing to do with the earthquake. I understood that my mind wanted to escape the space where horror kept it prisoner. Muffled laughter. I looked up. They're still talking in soft voices:

the grandmother and the grandson. A strong bond links these two beings separated by the abyss of time. They live in the same fluid universe of dreams. At the beginning and the end of life, we enjoy a time stripped of the responsibilities that weighed down our days. That free time allows old age and childhood to join hands. The grandmother is doing all she can to spare her grandson the horror of the day. Some people can dance on hot coals. People call them carefree and irresponsible, and don't understand that they are beings with exceptional souls. They pass through these times of suffering with steady hearts; they don't feel they need to add their personal anguish to the collective tragedy. My grandmother tore me from the claws of the dictator by teaching me something other than hatred and vengeance. This grandmother, on the other side of the net, is taking the horrible images in her grandson's head and replacing them with the songs and mythologies she can still find in her shaky memory.

*Taking Stock*

First thing in the morning, we get together to take stock of the situation. We can't continue in this lethargy. We have to do something—but what? The whole city's been through the blender. We're in a state of shock. The planet's eyes are riveted on Port-au-Prince. The images of destruction broadcast on a TV loop are stirring people's energy all around the world. The radio stations that have managed to get back on the air are spitting out horror stories. The Internet works intermittently, ten minutes at a time. The phones are still down. It's like the whole thing happened a thousand years ago. At the same time, we still haven't assimilated how bad the situation is. Even though I saw the bodies, I go on dreaming. I didn't describe the scenes to people who have stayed in the hotel. Figures are bandied about. It's all so abstract: 100,000 or 200,000. Add or subtract 10,000 dead, as if each death wasn't worthy of particular attention. All that is designed, of course, to keep you from going crazy. No one wants to be the first to go running naked down the street. We avoid considering reality, because reality is the problem.

*Rumors*

According to a rumor, the looting has already begun. Even in the hotel. Panic: it seems that someone has emptied the strong boxes in the rooms. In the courtyard and in front of the hotel, groups form to discuss the situation. We have to defend ourselves. We're not going to wait to have our throats cut like goats tied to a post. Voices are raised. People are exhausted. I go off and talk to the security guards. All clear there. Then the chambermaids. They've seen nothing out of the ordinary. The hotel owners? First time they've heard of such a thing. The strong boxes are all intact. That's how you kill a rumor before it spreads like oil on the glassy surface of a pond.

## City of Calm

In the end, there never were those chaotic scenes that some journalists (but not all) no doubt wanted to see. I could just picture the front page of a major daily paper if looting really had broken out. And the televised commentaries from the instant experts about this barbarous country. Instead, people saw a dignified nation whose nerves were steady enough to resist the most terrible deprivations. When you understand that people were hungry long before the earthquake, you have to wonder how they managed to wait so calmly for help to show up. What did they live on during the month that preceded the distribution of food? And the sick who wandered the streets of the city without treatment? Despite all that, Port-au-Prince never lost its cool. We saw people standing in line, waiting for bottled water in the slums, the same districts that a few months earlier were considered danger zones where the government's laws had no effect. So what happened? What can these changes be attributed to? Was this the shock the country was waiting for to wake up and halt its dizzying descent? We'll have to wait a while longer to understand the true impact of such a tremendous event on the nation's destiny. In the meantime, let's enjoy the calm. Especially since we know that explosions of another kind (social, this time) are on the horizon.

## Amos Oz

Just before I left for Haiti on January 5, when we were having dinner together, Saint-Éloi gave me a book: *The Same Sea* by Amos Oz. It was my first contact with a writer who has long attracted me. Since Saint-Éloi had brought his copy with him, we took out our two books to read Oz out loud. My confidence in poetry is unlimited. It alone can reconcile me with the horror of the world. Saint-Éloi read standing up. I was sitting on a suitcase. He thinks I have the same obsessions as Amos Oz: the relation with my mother, my village, and wandering. He read me these brief lines:

*… My view is different. Wandering is fitting for those who have lost their way. Kiss the feet my son of the woman Maria whose womb, for an instant, returned you to mine …*

I felt the small differences between us. My mother doesn't speak; she murmurs, like a song inside her. The voice of Amos Oz's mother seems surer. She orders him: *Kiss the feet my son of the woman Maria*. My mother doesn't know the imperative. Amos Oz's mother is a woman of passion; mine is one of gentleness.

*Washing Up*

Saint-Éloi goes with me. We fill a bucket of water from the pool. The bathroom is under the restaurant. No one outside of the hotel employees has ventured that far. We found two large towels near the pool. We don't go too far inside for fear of getting trapped in that narrow room if an aftershock were to strike. We rub ourselves vigorously to remove the stain of misfortune. We dry ourselves as we converse, like a couple of athletes after a tough game. We put on clean clothes and step outside. On the tennis court, I open my suitcase and take out my razor and aftershave. People watch us, surprised at first, then they get moving too, as if awakening from a nightmare. Michel Le Bris announces that he's going to wash his hair, and for the first time, he is willing to separate himself from his computer. He returns a few minutes later, a new man. The women bring out their lipstick. I exhibit my two mangos like war trophies. Which makes sense: when I went up to my room, I felt I was penetrating enemy territory. Someone hands me a jackknife. I offer everyone a thin slice of mango. It took an earthquake to get me to share a mango.

## The Decision

That ceremony had just ended when I saw people coming up from the other side of the fence. They were officials from the Canadian Embassy searching the hotels and offering a flight out to Canadian citizens who wanted to leave. The departure to the airport was scheduled for one p.m. from the Embassy. The decision had to be made immediately. Saint-Éloi couldn't go because he doesn't have Canadian citizenship. I wouldn't leave without him. I asked the officials to wait a minute. He and I went under a tree to talk it over. Stay or go—it's always the same dilemma. After a while, I went back to the Embassy staff and said I was going with them. I've learned to make up my mind fast. The same way I had to decide quickly during the first seconds of the earthquake. You have ten seconds to figure out whether you'll stay where you are or go elsewhere. That makes a difference, but I still wasn't completely sure I'd made the right decision. I hesitated between my heart that told me to stay with these people, and my mind that told me I would be more useful for them back there. In the end, I figured that this was probably the last time someone would offer to repatriate me.

*A Semantic Battle*

When I heard the question that a Canadian TV journalist asked me as I was walking across the tarmac at the Port-au-Prince airport, I understood that a new qualifier had been invented for

Haiti. For years, the country had been recognized as the first black republic in the world, and the second to win its independence in the Americas after the United States. Independence wasn't handed to us over martinis, after a few hypocritical smiles and pompous speeches on a lawn littered with confetti. It was won after an armed struggle against the greatest European army at the time led by Napoleon Bonaparte. My childhood was filled with stories of slaves whose only weapon was their longing for freedom and a senseless kind of bravery. On summer evenings, my grandmother would tell me of the exploits of our heroes who had to take everything from the enemy, weapons and the art of war, for starters. Even the French language was part of "the spoils of war." Then suddenly, toward the end of the 1980s, people started talking about Haiti only in terms of poverty and corruption. A country is never corrupt—but its ruling class can be. The three-quarters of the population that, despite endemic poverty, manage to keep their dignity, should not be subjected to that insult. When outsiders talk about Haiti, those three-quarters feel concerned, and when the country is insulted, they—not the rich—feel the sting. The poorest country, no doubt, since the figures say so. But does that wipe away our history? People accuse us of dwelling on it. But no more than any other country. When a French TV network wants to fill its coffers, it airs yet another series about Napoleon. Think of the number of films and books about the history of France or England or even the Vietnam War, whereas there hasn't been a single film about the greatest colonial war of all time, the one that allowed slaves to become citizens through sheer willpower. And now here comes a new label that is going to bury us completely: Haiti is a cursed country. Some Haitians, at the end of their rope, are even starting to believe it. You have to be really desperate to accept the contempt that others have for you. The only place to fight that label is where it germinated: in Western opinion. My sole argument: what did this country do to deserve its curse? I know a country that started two world wars in one century and proposed a final solution, and no one says it's cursed. I know a country insensitive to human suffering, that continues to starve the planet from its powerful financial centers, and no one says it's cursed. On the contrary: it claims to be a nation blessed by the gods—by God, more like it. So why would Haiti be cursed? I suppose some people use that label in good faith, finding no other words to name this stream of misfortune. But it's not the right word, especially when you see the energy and dignity displayed by the nation as it faces one of the most difficult tests of our time. But each passing day makes the fight harder. All some commentator has to do is say the word "curse" on the airwaves and it spreads like a cancer. Before they can move on to voodoo, wild men, cannibalism, and a nation of blood-drinkers, they'll see that I have enough energy to fight them.

*A Night of Distress*

I landed in Montreal in the middle of the night. My wife couldn't come and get me at the airport. Some people I met drove me home. She seemed as exhausted as I was. The last few days must have been terrible for her. For one night and one morning, I had completely dropped off her radar. That had never happened before. She didn't know any more than the journalists who kept calling to find out how I was. She had no idea where I was, if I was at the hotel or elsewhere. Or dead. At 4:53 in the afternoon, a person can be anywhere. I had tried several times during the night to reach her. The telephone rang but no one answered. She told me she felt it was me, but she didn't hear anything. An emptiness. As if the call were coming from another world. I was frightened when I heard that, since she's never been superstitious. Her only obsession is protecting her private life. I hardly ever talk about her in public for more than a few minutes. And she found herself having to manage two major crises at the same time: my disappearance and the media. Most journalists were thoughtful, she told me, even if there was a little misunderstanding at one point. She couldn't understand that the fact of not knowing where I might be was news in itself. One journalist asked my wife's permission to record her words. She kept saying that she had nothing to say because she didn't know where I was. In the end, the poor journalist understood that my wife didn't know that absurd system according to which nothing can be news. Then night came. But not sleep. Next to her, the telephone was silent. She couldn't concentrate on her crossword puzzles. She's probably thinking that I'm talking about her too much, and not enough about the people who lost their families. But I'm really talking about the anxiety that runs through the veins of anyone waiting for a phone call. I remember the last lines of the poem "Nuit d'hôpital" by Roussan Camille as he is waiting for dawn in a hospital bed in Port-au-Prince: "Our Lady of Fevers, mistress of anguish, have pity on the thoughts that run to madness in the night."

## The Small Screen

Inside Haiti, we didn't have enough perspective to see the big picture. We could only take care of those next to us and had no idea what was happening in other parts of the city. The radio wasn't working full-time yet. We had to find water, help an injured person get to the hospital, look after a child whose parents had disappeared. Everyone was trying to find out if their family members were still all alive. We didn't dare ask if people had survived. It's always a shock to learn of a friend's death. In Haiti, we experienced all that first-hand, but in only one place at a time (the place we happened to be). From outside the country, we had a panoramic view of the city. The small screen never blinks. A protean eye made of hundreds of cameras that show everything. Everything is naked. Flattened out. Death without discretion, since the camera, at first, made no distinction between class and gender. Since I returned a few hours ago, I've been lying prostrate on the bed, watching an endless parade of horrifying images, unable to absorb the fact that I've just emerged from that landscape of devastation. The worst thing is not this succession of misfortunes, but the absence of all nuance in the camera's cold eye. Sleep came and caressed the back of my neck, warning me it was time to let go.

## A Glass of Water

I woke up bathed in sweat. I felt the room moving. The books on the bedside table had fallen to the floor, carrying the telephone with them. I must have been having a nightmare and knocked over the glass of water with my hand. I always keep a glass of water next to me because I often get up in the middle of the night to read. Mostly poetry. The little mess I'd made affected me because I know people don't have enough water in Haiti. And what they have, they have to boil. It's not easy to start a fire when you can't find matches. I think of all those smokers trapped in a city without cigarettes. What's worse, the Barbancourt company that makes the local rum sustained major damage. I stare at the wet floor and can't stop picturing the faces of thirsty people. Normally I'm against transposing torment from one place to another. It's better to keep your energy to help people solve their problems. Just because there's a water shortage in Port-au-Prince doesn't mean there should be one in Montreal. I lift myself and slide the pillow behind my head. I turn on the TV without the sound. The images flicker by in silence. A continuous stream. Women with arms raised skyward. Long lines of people walking with no destination. A girl telling a story I don't need to hear to understand. I drift off again and leave the TV on. Turning it off would be like slamming the door on all those people who demand our attention. In any case, the telephone next to my head never sleeps.

*Year Zero*

I turned on the TV this morning and found myself listening to a political analyst who claims that Haiti could get back on its feet again if the country agreed to forget everything that occurred before the earthquake. He spoke of life before the event, which was hardly paradise. The scene was shocking, since the analyst and the journalist interviewing him were comfortably seated while behind them, in full screen, pictures of desolation streamed past. Just look at those scenes of horror (screaming faces that make no sound) and you're bound to agree with everything being said. This technique of intimidation is so widespread we don't see anything abnormal about it. What's happening is this: we're presented with a problem while being prevented from truly thinking about it. The answer is behind the question. To wrap up everything in a single expression supposedly rich with hope, the expert calls it "Year Zero." Zorro to the rescue. It's the first time I've heard the concept of Year Zero applied to Haiti. I can't swallow the idea despite the intolerable images that assault my eye. After all this time, people should know you can't erase the memory of a nation so easily. In Haiti's case, history begins with the prodigious leap from Africa to America. People driven by a desperate desire to live together, despite the many reasons that would dissuade them from doing just that, are what creates cities, not the other way around. The earthquake didn't destroy Port-au-Prince; no one can build a new city without thinking of the old. The human landscape counts. Its memory will link the old and the new. Nothing is ever begun from scratch. It's impossible, in any case. All we do is continue. There are things you can never eliminate from a trajectory, like human sweat. What should be done with the two centuries, and all they contain, that preceded Year Zero? Throw it all in the garbage? A culture that pays attention only to the living risks its own death.

*My Mother on the Phone*

I finally reached my mother on the phone. Her voice was clear, but always with that trace of concern. She was happy to hear from me. The evening before I left, thinking I was going to come back, she made me something to eat, and that missed meal saddened me. Like every time, the conversation got around to her health, which worries me. To reassure me, she told me her appetite has returned. I picture her picking at a few grains of rice, like a bird. My doubts reached her over the phone. She can read my states of mind, even from a distance. She handed the phone to my sister, who confirmed she was eating more lately. What is she eating? Mostly the sweets you send her, she says with a side order of blame. My sister and I have opposing opinions on the subject. She'd like my mother to eat filling food: rice, beans in sauce, chicken. Which my mother refuses, because she only wants to eat sweet things. Otherwise, all she'll tolerate, when it comes to *filling*, is spaghetti and peanut butter. She's practically allergic to rice and red beans; she's eaten them every day for the last eighty years. It does me good to talk about the small details of daily life with my sister: those little things mean life has returned. After a silence (her silences always fill me with dread), she gave the phone to my nephew who provided me with a complete description of everything that's happened since the earthquake. He travels throughout the city; he's my source of information. He told me about Filo's misadventure, which he considers comical. Apparently, there was a passageway behind the wide black curtain I saw in the studio. Filo wormed his way into it and was able to crawl free of the building before it collapsed. His gods didn't images random or do the news directors know from experience what will move their audience? All that work in the flow of the moment. I try to see something new. Like that woman moving through the crowd. The way she's walking, with no sense of anxiety, gives no idea of her destination. She's just *there*. The truth is that people are in no hurry any more because most of them have lost their houses. They have no decent place to live, so they live in the moment.

*Ten Seconds*

She came and sat next to me on the yellow sofa. Slender and refined, she was extremely careful how she broached the subject. She wanted to know if there was a moment when I lost my head, knowing I might die. That isn't a question to be taken lightly. I took my time answering. I think what helped, I told her, is that we were together as a group. There were three of us. We supported each other. I don't know how I would have acted if the earthquake had caught me alone in my room. If the question had been, "Were you afraid?" I would have said Yes, but not at the beginning. The first violent tremor took me completely by surprise. No time to think. I was afraid when the second tremor shook us; it was almost as strong as the first. It came just as I was getting my thoughts back. Just when I figured I'd made it through, the second shock was like a blow to the back of the head. I understood this thing was serious. This was no play: the actors weren't going to get back up for the applause. There was no audience. No one would escape unharmed. For ten seconds, I waited for death. Wondering what form it would take. Would the earth gape open and swallow us up? Would the trees fall on us? Fire consume us? At that moment, I knew I couldn't stay distant from it. In any case, I wasn't up to it. If an earthquake could shake an entire city, one individual was not going to resist it. That's when we cling to our most archaic beliefs. We think of the gods of the earth. I waited and waited. Nothing. I got to my feet, humbly. I felt the worst was behind me. But for ten seconds, those horrible ten seconds, I lost what I had so carefully accumulated all my life. The veneer of civilization that I'd been inculcated with went up in smoke—a cloud of dust like the ruins of the city. All that took ten seconds. Is that the true weight of civilization? During those ten seconds, I was a tree, a rock, a cloud, or the earthquake itself. One thing was for sure: I wasn't the product of a culture any more. I had the definite impression of being part of the cosmos. The most precious seconds of my life. I don't really know if there was a gap of ten seconds, but I'm sure the emotions were real. We all shared the same event, but we didn't experience it the same way.

*Sharing*

You turn on the TV and feel their presence. They're the first volunteers who found a seat in a plane. They don't give their opinions; they act. I watch them file out of the plane and head immediately in the right direction. They know where to go. The situation is tailor-made for them. Most of them come from the United States: Adventists, Baptists. The Creole that their leaders learned in American universities makes it possible for them to fan out rapidly throughout the country. Traditionally, the Catholic church took the side of the political, cultural, and economic elite, and the Protestants used that fact to infiltrate the overall population. The Protestants vigorously pursued the war against voodoo that the Catholics began in the 1940s with their famous anti-superstition campaign. Over the last decades, the Catholic church has understood that to survive, it would have to win the heart of the poorer classes. Nowadays, you can't tell the Catholics apart from the Protestants, since the two wolves have the same attitude toward the flock. Then you have to factor in the humanitarian organizations that act like left-wing clergy. They claim to be more practical and direct, but they're just as emotionally manipulative. In the end, there's no difference. Those who practice voodoo, who were always considered archaic, have been trying to modernize. They use the Internet and cell phones and want to claim their share of the market by tinkling the bell of nationalism. The people have all the opium they need. If the day ever comes when there's enough to eat, will they still want to smoke so much?

*Staggering Steps*

I panic when I think I might have absorbed a dose of anxiety strong enough to remain in my body. A month after the earthquake, I'm still sensitive to the slightest vibration. Is the information rooted in my mind or my body? I'd like to know what triggers panic: my head or my body? The other evening, I was eating with friends when I felt something. A slight vibration at first, then it grew in intensity. Unbelievable: the other people just went on with their conversation. I was about to make a dash for the door when I realized the guy next to me was tapping his knee against the table—a nervous tic. Once, when I was on the fif-teenth floor of a building downtown, I had the very strong feel-ing that everything was going to collapse in a matter of seconds. When I looked out the window, I was sure the building across the street was moving. The more solid a place seems, the less confi-dent I am. Just now, as I was writing those lines, the chair moved. All rationality fled my body, and I was alone with my panic. And what about the people whose nightmare still continues? I'm talking about the ones who didn't have the means to leave the island. I can't imagine what it's like to walk upon ground that has already betrayed you.

*The Pivotal Moment*

This event will have repercussions as important as those caused by the declaration of Haitian independence on January 1, 1804. At the time of independence, the Western world turned its back on the new republic and it had to enjoy its triumph alone. That was the destiny of a nation that had just left behind the long, black, suffocating tunnel of slavery. The West refused to recog-nize its emergence onto the world stage. Europe and America alike turned their backs. Mad with solitude, these new free men devoured each other like beasts. Ever since, the West has pointed to Haiti as an example for anyone who wants to free himself from slavery without its permission. The punishment has lasted for over two centuries. You will be free, but alone. Nothing is worse than being alone on an island. And now every eye turns to Haiti. I picture an enormous door slowly turning on hinges of darkness and light. A pivotal moment. During the last two weeks of January 2010, Haiti was seen more often than during the previous two centuries. And it wasn't because of a coup or one of those bloody stories mixing voodoo and cannibalism—it was because of an earthquake. An event over which no one has any control. For once, our misfortune wasn't exotic. What happened to us could have happened anywhere.

*The Desire to Help*

In the streets of Montreal, I can measure the depth of emotion set off by Haiti's misfortune. People seem moved to their very souls, as if the city were one with Haiti. I went home and saw those inconsolable faces again on TV (always in close-up).

Nurses rushing off to help the injured, children raising funds by any means possible (selling their art and putting on shows) and delivering it to humanitarian organizations, amateur and professional musicians sending the totality of their proceeds from their concerts to orphanages, suburban rockers with Mohawk haircuts wearing T-shirts with "I Love Haiti" printed on them, journalists who want to adopt the children they hold in their arms for the camera, giant benefits like in the days of "We Are the World" that raise dozens of millions of dollars in a single night, Hollywood stars who sell their party dresses and buy food with the money, big names from the movies who use their personal airplanes to ferry in medicine, doctors who operate until they're exhausted. Not to mention anonymous individuals who want to act, but discreetly and modestly. But where is all this energy going? And where is all the money ending up? People want to help so much that they don't try to find out the answers. The sadness on their faces alternates with the will to really do something. And do it personally. Haiti has barged into their private lives.

*The Last Doctor*

I watch my mother putting the utensils back on the shelves. The tablecloths in the drawers. The baskets, blue and pink plastic, carefully lined up on the counter. She insists on doing the household chores even though she has a wound on her right leg that won't heal. Her doctor died in the earthquake, and she needs a new one fast. It's not easy, since everyone wants an appointment. People injured in the earthquake have priority, especially those in danger for their lives. Last month, so many arms and legs were amputated that could have been saved in other circumstances. Now, people are afraid of this bush medicine where everything is done at top speed. At the beginning, there weren't enough drugs, especially antibiotics, and doctors feared gangrene like the plague. A good number of Haitian doctors became unavailable; their own families needed their help. Then there were the ones who were injured or killed. What can you do but turn to Jesus, the only real doctor, as my mother says, whose clinic is open day and night. It's remarkable that Haitians aren't cursing God for this endless river of misfortune. Are they too weak or too resigned to find the energy to shake their fists at the sky? They do it sometimes, in their way. My sister told me that one of her girlfriends, who used to go to mass with her every morning, hasn't gone since January 12. "Why not?" my sister wanted to know. "It's up to Jesus to come and visit me—he needs to ask forgiveness." That made everyone laugh but my mother.

*The Energy of Things*

In this city, people bring everything outside every day. Since every house is also a store, in the morning they set out the merchandise on the sidewalk. When evening comes, they bring it all back in. They even bring in the counters on which the merchandise is displayed. It's amazing to see how many things can be stowed in a tiny house. In the empty streets at night, all you come across are large skeletal dogs.

*A Feminine Universe*

It took four heart attacks to kill Aunt Renée. The woman looked so frail, but she resisted and fought till the end. She always did her exercises until she was physically unable to. Nothing that happened in the house escaped her radar. Often, in the afternoon, she would sit on the gallery with my mother. Now my mother seems more fragile than ever. Over the last years, I've lost three of my four aunts. Of the women, only the youngest is left, Aunt Ninine, and the eldest, my mother. I told Aunt Ninine that a duel was brewing between her and my mother, between the youngest and the oldest. My joke turned Aunt Ninine gloomy. Of all my aunts, Renée was the most secretive.

*The Guilty Party*

My sister, my mother, and I slept on the gallery. Last month, the women were sleeping on mattresses in the yard. They suspect that's what finished off Aunt Renée. That, and the lack of care. Before the earthquake, medicine was hard to find. When you went to the hospital, you had to bring your own. In this country, you don't go there until the pain becomes unbearable. Otherwise, you don't consider yourself sick. It's better not to be sick if you can't pay for the medicine. That way, you go from being in good health to being dead. Illness is a luxury you can't afford if you don't have the means. So you die without ever having been sick. Death is always sudden. Since that kind of death has no scientific explanation, it becomes mysterious. Finally, we have a guilty party: the earthquake. On its slate, besides all those who perished in the rubble, we should add everyone who died from lack of medical care. The months following the event were so hard that people died of hunger and cold. The nights weren't warm enough for frail constitutions. Like Aunt Renée's.

*On the Gallery*

Yesterday evening, my mother's face was dark with sadness. Her foot had swelled up again. I put her legs on a pile of pillows and went and sat on Aunt Renée's narrow bed. My mother closed her eyes. She's not afraid of pain; immobility is what frightens her. She's never stood still in her life. I did what I do every time: I slipped a 100-*gourde* note under Aunt Renée's pillow. My mother opened her eyes, saw me, and smiled. The last time I was in this room with Aunt Renée, my nephew came and got her for her bath. She lay light and smiling in his arms. Once so prudish, she wasn't afraid to be seen naked. I heard voices. My female cousins had arrived to discuss the funeral. We sat on the gallery. Should there be a mass in Creole, French, or even Latin? My mother came out and joined us. One of my cousins insisted on Latin because it's more prestigious. But the choir was quickly rejected because it's too expensive. We decided a soloist would do just as well. There's one woman who sings very well, but her price is out of reach. One of my cousins went to school with her younger sister. We quickly gave up on that idea because, ever since she's become a star, the TV follows her everywhere. Impossible to imagine a camera at Aunt Renée's funeral—she who, all her life, avoided making any noise at all. My sister thought that discussing these kind of details was too painful when people were still searching for their families in the wreckage. One of my cousins replied that the earthquake didn't kill Aunt Renée, and that my sister shouldn't mix things up. My mother, her eyes still closed, began to murmur Aunt Renée's favorite prayer: "The angel of the Lord encampeth round about them that fear him, and delivereth them." I remember the intensity with which Aunt Renée would say "and delivereth them."

## A Young Christ

A large portrait of Christ on the gallery. It hung in my brother-in-law's school that collapsed in the earthquake. While he was transporting everything he could save in a truck, the portrait dropped onto the street. Someone found it and took it home. A passerby told my brother-in-law what had happened and pointed out the person's house. It took a lot of negotiations to get the portrait back. My mother has always liked this particular portrait of Jesus with his clear eyes and little pink mouth. Wavy hair cascading to his shoulders. His well-tended beard, strangely split in the middle. The index finger of his right hand strokes a flaming heart girdled by a crown of thorns. A soothing light forms the background. My mother looks that way every time she sits on the gallery.

## The Street-Corner Prophet

Just about everyone wakes up together in Port-au-Prince with the early morning sun. I go and brush my teeth in the yard. A light breeze carries an aroma of coffee. My sister wants to go food shopping, and I go along. People still greet one another like before, despite the trials of daily life. They sleep next to their houses. I see tents everywhere. A group of young students chatting under a tree. Everyone else hurrying to work. The camp on my left occupies a soccer field. Already sweating, adults emerge from the tents, holding the hands of their children swathed in colorful uniforms. Well-groomed, white socks, and polished shoes. Two men prepare to cross the street with a mattress on their heads. My sister slows to let them go by. This is new, I say to her; people never used to brake for pedestrians. My sister smiles. Red light. A man next to the car is shouting: we haven't seen anything yet, the end of days is near. Only the blind can't see the signs. A man walking by asks him ironically what the next step is going to be. A tsunami, he says very seriously. But before that, he adds, we'll have another earthquake two times stronger and three times longer than the last one, and it'll knock everything down and help the tsunami wipe out all trace of our existence here. This land doesn't belong to us. We're just renters. The owner lives upstairs, he says, pointing to the sky. And he's disappointed with our behavior. Instead of thanking him, all we do is fornicate and backbite. We don't have to pay rent; all he asks of us is to recognize him as our Lord and God. Instead we're too busy worshiping the Golden Calf. A few people stop to listen to him, mostly women. Green light. The car pulls away, leaving the prophet to gesticulate under the lamp post.

and movie stars instead. What has my sister worried is the brief article that predicts gasoline shortages because of the strike in Venezuela, our only supplier. The Dominican Republic is ready to help out, but how long can they last? Further on in the story, there's a warning that prices are going to go through the roof. My sister wants to get back home and park the car.

*The House across the Way*

I'm sitting on the gallery. My mother slipped a pillow behind my neck and patted my shoulder. I drift toward sleep. Kids are playing soccer next door. I hear their laughter. The shrill voices of the street vendors. The joyful shouts when a goal is scored. The big house across the way that used to block our view fell down. The woman who owned the house was pulled out from underneath the stairway. Her son was part of the rescue team. She spent her whole life slaving away in New York to be able to build the place. She showed up every December and added a room, then went back to work in May. From the gallery, my mother followed the progress of the work as the years went by. It's strange that the house, the envy of the neighborhood, was the only one that didn't hold up. Now we can see the mountains it once hid. All day long, people speculate on why some houses stood the test while others, right next door, collapsed. Some people believe that Goudougoudou (the name that the poorer parts of town gave the earthquake, since this was the sound people heard) acted intentionally. A new god has been born. Not in the sense of a god who punishes; he's been named to give him an identity. The way it's done with hurricanes.

## Aunt Renée's Funeral

We were all ready early since, as family members, we have to be at the church before everyone else. My mother is elegantly dressed, with a slight smile that worries me instead of reassuring me, which is what she wants to do. I help her into the car. She taps me on the shoulder to thank me, which she never does. My sister tried in vain to get her to eat something before going to the church, since right after the funeral we're driving to Petit-Goâve to bury Aunt Renée in the cemetery there, where she'll join her sisters and brother. My mother decided not to listen to anyone today. She wanted to spend this time with her sister.

Watching her, so serene, I sense she's caught up to her somewhere in their childhood. My mother sat up very straight in the church. A determined look in her eye that I hadn't seen for some time. Instead of crushing her (when Aunt Raymonde died, she denied the fact so completely that I thought she'd lost her mind), Aunt Renée's death has had the opposite effect. The celebrant had a reassuring presence too—he was Aunt Renée's confessor. Over the final months, he would come to the house to give her communion, Sunday morning after the last mass. He's from Petit-Goâve as well and, naturally, he'll be accompanying us there. I spotted relatives I thought were dead. They gave us news of our extended family. We lost several members to the earthquake, people I didn't know. The church is full. I'm surprised that Aunt Renée, who never left the house and was bedridden the last twenty years of her life, could have known so many people. I'm told that they too lost family in the earthquake, and now they're attending the funerals of people they don't know to pay tribute to their own dead. Once mass is over, they come to offer their condolences. We could have offered ours. We have all lost someone. My mother is holding up well. She stands straight, and her eyes are steady. I don't dare touch her for fear that her scaffolding will collapse. My sister goes to get the car; she'll pick us up in front of the church. We start out for Petit-Goâve. Improvised camps line both sides of the road. I can't imagine what will happen when it was all. Zweig may be a little precious, but he's not necessarily worldly. His sad inner monologues and deleterious atmospheres created a state of total dependence in a passionate reader like Aunt Renée. I wonder whether Zweig's toxic prose turned my aunt into a melancholy being, or whether her melancholy drove her to Zweig. How was it that such a sad creature appeared in our family in which everyone loved celebration? I must confess that, though I'm not sad myself, sadness has always intrigued me. What struck me was the respect she earned through it. As if her natural delicacy of feeling conferred a kind of grace to our town. Yet her life was lived according to strict ritual. She went to the library in the morning and returned to the house in the afternoon. I remember her colorful parasols, her only touch of fantasy, that sheltered her from the implacable four o'clock sun when she went to visit Dr Cayemite's dispensary for her medicines. I always felt that people sought to protect her from the vulgarity of daily life. As if Aunt Renée represented that nobler part of themselves they could be proud of. As I watched her, I understood that pain in its constancy had profoundly shaped her personality. Her breathing, shallow as if she were gasping for air, gave her a particular winged way of moving—that was pain showing itself. Yet she stubbornly concealed her suffering. I remember that when the pain got too intense, she would go and lie down on the couch in the shadowy living room. She would stay there an hour or two trees, a dance floor where they had set up a long table covered in a white cloth. The family's teenage girls served us. Now and again, someone took me aside discreetly to give me an account of everything that had happened in Petit-Goâve since I left in 1963. Naturally, I knew none of the names that were mentioned, but what touched me was the gravity with which these sagas were told. I didn't know how to react, because I wasn't sure what these people were getting at. We just want to talk to you, one of my cousins said. We don't see you very often. At the end of the story, they shook my hand and held it, gazing into my eyes. I turned away in the face of such intensity. Calloused, peasant hands that left a smell of green leaves. City people smell like gasoline. The difference in smells separates us. We are all related in these little towns where cousins marry each other. I joined the rest of the group that was laughing as they told a story about Aunt Renée. After coffee and a last glass of rum, we went into the town, and I lingered by the harbor. The church, where I once waited on the steps for my teacher Mr Calonges, who gave me private lessons, is now a ruin. The library across the way, where I gave a talk last December, is just a memory. Not a stone standing. As I stood by the presbytery, I could see the water. On the way back, I met a young doctor working for the Red Cross. He told me in no uncertain terms that malaria had made a dramatic return to the region. Since I hadn't taken my pills before I left on this trip, I

*A Body Quake*

A friend invited me to a restaurant. Night was falling. We heard whispering nearby. A swarm of humans moving inside their tents. A few lamps lit. As we climbed toward Pétionville, we saw how much it had rained. We reached the place Saint-Pierre. I wondered how these people manage to sleep in the mud, night after night, with the rainwater that comes sweeping down the mountain. Fortunately, the sun dries everything out during the day. We went by a discotheque. Line-ups of luxury cars. People have come here to let go after all their trials. The restaurant is perched on a hill with a magnificent view of the city. I see people up there and wonder what it must be like, eating as you look out on a broken city. My friend took me to La Plantation where the fish is very good. Just before dessert, I went into the bathroom to rinse my face when my legs gave out. I grabbed onto the sink. I felt a good strong shock. My breath gone. Sweating already. I sat down on the toilet. My legs were weak. I went back to the table once I'd gotten hold of myself. The same atmosphere as before. Nothing indicated there'd been a tremor. I can't be the only one who felt it. People are going to mention it. I just need to wait. The conversations were as lively as ever. Finally I understood that my body had shaken, not the earth.

## A New Word

I'm standing on the sidewalk, waiting for my nephew to come back. Young women slip out of their tents in the camp next door. They're dressed for Saturday night. My nephew is late, and my mother is worried. I listen to the radio that she forgot on the gallery by her chair. Actually, I'm not really listening. You can't count the number of radio stations in Port-au-Prince. I recognize them by their decibel level. A lot of announcers think they have to scream to get the public's attention. Their voices add to the heat. Other announcers present a more distinguished profile to charm the upper-class audiences who hate those loud, demanding voices. Really, I'm not as bothered as I let on by the cacophony of everyone shouting out his argument without even pretending to listen to anyone else. Politics is the only subject, the daily bread of those who prefer opinion to information. Despite the noise, it's a kind of barometer. Someone has just burst into flames of wrathful anger—then I realize it's only theater. From the inflamed discussions, I've picked out these words (shouted every time) that keep coming back: cracks, ruins, reconstruction, camps, tents, provisions. Will they dislodge the words from the previous generation: Aristide, *les chimères*, corruption, de facto government, eradication, and embargo? Or the terms from the generation before: Duvalier, dictatorship, prison, exile, *tonton-macoute*. Every decade has its vocabulary. The frequency of certain words in the media informs us about the state of things. For many years, the two favorite ones were "dictatorship" and "corruption." Now, for the first time, we're hearing "reconstruction." That's a new one. Even if most people can't really believe it.

## A Slight Indisposition

My mother and my sister were on the gallery. My nephew was working on his political economy homework. I was on the bed in his room. My brother-in-law was eating dinner alone with his newspaper. Suddenly, we heard a dish shatter. My nephew jumped up and discovered my brother-in-law stretched out on the table, his jaws locked. We didn't know what to do. My sister walked calmly into the room. Her cool demeanor always scares me because I know, deep down, that she's panicking. She threw cold water on my brother-in-law's face. I worked to loosen the grip of his jaw as my nephew tried to slip an aspirin into his mouth. It was no use. A little sugar water was more effective. He'd felt ill suddenly, and thinking his blood pressure was too high, he took a drug to lower it. But the opposite happened. A quick drop in blood pressure threw him into a kind of coma. My mother's face was a picture of concentration as she paced the corridor, calling upon the Virgin's help. Once the crisis passed, my nephew started making jokes, but we knew he was afraid. We all went off to bed without any more discussion. My nephew plugged in the machine that keeps away mosquitoes. We listened to the dry buzz of grilling mosquitoes until my sister asked him to turn the thing off so we could sleep.

## Frankétienne's Strategy

I went by Frankétienne's place yesterday. He wasn't there. I looked around the garden. Everything seemed to be in good order, including the disorder. This morning I saw the stone-masons at work. The foreman invited me to look around; Frankétienne wanted me to, though he couldn't be here today because he had a meeting out of town. Once a month, he meets with old friends for long discussions on a variety of subjects. In other words, he wouldn't be back until evening. I noticed solid-looking steel poles planted here and there, better to resist the next earthquake. Frankétienne had painted them in the Basquiat style. I detected echoes of the two Haitian painters closest to him, Tiga and Saint-Brice. That's Frankétienne in a nutshell: he sees the world as an artist does. I wouldn't mention it to the foreman, but if you ask me, adding steel poles is not going to make the house more resistant to earthquakes. The opposite is true. But Frankétienne is a maximalist. Faced with an earthquake, the best strategy is to bend so you don't break, but he reinforced his backbone with concrete. The next time will be a duel. But what matters most is that he's trying to turn this disaster into a work of art.

## Wood

People have started talking about wood again. I remember that before the earthquake, the problem of clear-cutting was on the agenda. That's all anyone talked about, especially in the international media. Haiti was on the brink of ecological disaster. No trees, so nothing to hold down the arable land when the hard rains fell. You could literally see the bones of the country. That's because people cut down the trees to make charcoal. In recent years, every presidential candidate added tree-planting to their program. If there are any trees left standing, it's because concrete has become the favorite building material. But since it failed the earthquake test, the latest talk is of going back to wood, since it's more flexible and resisted the tremors better than cement. That's true enough, but if we go back to wood, we'll risk ecological catastrophe.

## My Nomadic Friend

My friend Dominique Batraville lives in Port-au-Prince, but I don't have his address. In any case, he's never home. I always meet him at an art show, a book launch, or a press conference at the Ministry of Culture. He's a cultural journalist, exactly what I did when I lived here. He's part of the group of young poets that my brother-in-law Christophe Charles published a few decades ago in his magazine, which featured only poets eighteen years old or younger. His first collection of poems in Creole, *Boulpic*, was a great success. Like many in his generation, he went through hell without a complaint. When I ask after his health, he'll slap his chest with his open palm: his way of reassuring me. His way of defying his illness, too. You never know what shape he'll be in when you see him. He has his ups and downs. When things are going really bad, he'll disappear from sight for a month or more. Alarmed, his friends go looking for him, though they know he'll reappear on his own one day. And suddenly he's there. You can hear his characteristic laugh from a distance. One of the few men I know who has no enemies. You should never say something like that, but I say it in his case. He crosses borders effortlessly in a country where social classes are no laughing matter. He's a jack-of-all-trades: radio host, newspaper journalist, poet, actor, and volunteer impresario. Often you see him with a talented young artist he's promoting. He travels the city. You picture him ever more fragile, especially since his mother's death. When he catches my concerned look, he gives me a wink of reassurance. While Frankétienne watches Port-au-Prince from the balcony of his house where he stands bare-chested, Batraville moves through the city on foot. He knows every part of it. With his way of covering the territory, he reminds me of Gasner Raymond, my friend who was murdered by the dictatorship thirty-five years ago. Gasner was positively caustic. Although Batraville's laugh might seem sarcastic at times, you can tell right away that he's a generous, gentle man. You can feel it by the way he opens his arms wide when he goes to greet you—he does it with his whole body. I breathed easier when I learned he had survived the earthquake. In his precarious state, the man sums up this untamable city.

*A Photo*

In this broken place, a lot of people who have come to help brought their cameras with them. At first they try to capture the suffering on film. The pictures are sent to their friends via the Internet. Then, after a while, they begin to enjoy it. Every photo creates a certain amount of interest back home. And every amateur photographer dreams of being in the right place at the right time to get a great picture. They imitate the professionals by shooting away at everything and anything. I met one of those amateurs happily shooting blindly into the crowd. He told me he was taking a photo class at a Miami university with an old-school teacher who accepts paper photos only, which cost him a fortune. Be spontaneous, no framing, give me untouched reality. The teacher tears up the pictures so quickly you wonder if he took the time to look at them. He told me all about his class as he went on shooting. I watched him and realized his method is not much different from his teacher's. And wondered who was taking the photo: he or the camera? Why didn't he take the time to look at the person he was photographing? What is this need to shoot people blindly? As if any picture will do. The look he gave me made me realize we weren't living in the same century. It takes me at least an hour to photograph a scene, but with his machine, he can take fifty a minute. I look like an old artisan with my black notebook in which I write down every detail that will help me sketch out a face. We followed the crowds and ended up on the square in front of the ruined cathedral. We went on talking about our different art forms and our respective methods. He seemed more receptive than before, making mental calculations to see how much he could save with this technique of a single photo. Still, there's something seductive about a photographer shooting multiple pictures of the same subject. I don't know what a writer at work looks like. We came across a woman standing with her arms thrown open in front of a great black cross—all that remains of the cathedral. I sat down on a low wall to write. How to describe a scene like that? He took just one picture.


## New Landmarks

The government can name streets if it wants to, but people have their own way of establishing landmarks. A church, an empty house, a park, a public building, a stadium, a cemetery—anything can be a landmark. People invent their own personal map of the city. They come from the countryside with precise information that will help them locate a family member or friend. Luckily, no one building looks like another, and no urban plan was ever considered. Everyone had his say when it came to building his house so it wouldn't look like a rabbit hutch. Every house can be found thanks to its originality and especially its loud colors. But when everything has been destroyed, and since people have always refused to orient themselves according to street names, it's a little hard to get your bearings, especially at first. That situation created a new reality and people had to adapt fast. "You know where the Caribbean Market used to be? Well, you go past it, and then two buildings that collapsed..." To the landscape of this crumbled city, people have added elements of the old one still present in their memory. For the population whose minds are always in ferment, things accumulate instead of disappearing. We'll have to wait for a generation who never knew the old city, and who'll be willing to accept a new map.

*Golf*

For the last few months, the golf course has been occupied by a crowd of people who knew nothing about the game before the earthquake. The game is hard to comprehend in a city so over-populated. It takes up too much space for too few people: no more than a dozen bored spouses and young mistresses who pretend to be amused as they wait for the game to end. A tiny white ball for such a vast surface—it seems like another provocation. And the players take their time in a country where the abbreviated life expectancy pushes people into constant agitation. Anyway, soccer is our passion. The land is good, but there's not a single fruit tree in sight. Most agronomists believe that our survival can be credited to the mango and avocado trees that serve as a rampart against famine. The owners of the golf course are getting worried; they sense that the crowd is not about to leave the grounds. It took an earthquake to get them here, and it will take an event of equal magnitude to chase them away.

## The Chair

Between Aunt Renée's and my mother's bed, in the narrow room, stands a chair. It's an old chair that my grandmother brought from Petit-Goâve. It reminds me that my grandmother, before she died, shared this room with my Aunt Renée. My mother slept in the room where my sister is now. After my grandmother's death, my mother came and replaced her, next to Aunt Renée. She couldn't be left alone at night after her heart attack. The room is Spartan, with two single beds separated by an old chest of drawers. And the chair where I would sit when I wanted to spend time with them. Actually, I used the chair to converse with my mother. When I talked to Aunt Renée, I preferred to sit on the bed. I was the only one to whom she granted that privilege. After her illness began, she had trouble expressing herself, and you had to be close to her to understand. My mother knew her so well she could anticipate her every desire even before she spoke it. The other family members did their best to decipher the noises she made. But since I was rarely there, I had to concentrate on her face (her mouth and eyes) to understand her. She repeated every word several times, with a touching kind of patience, until I understood what she was trying to say. Often it was the same thing: news of my daughters, how my health was, the subject of the book I was writing. We clung to these conversations and refused all intermediaries (starting with my mother) who would have served as translators. After a conversation with Aunt Renée, I would sit on the chair, taking my place between the two women who occupied such an important place in my life, and in my writing as well. The chair, like the room itself, has aged, but my mother doesn't see it that way. She wants my sister to have it repaired. And when my mother really wants something, she'll talk about it day and night. My sister is in a tough spot. She can't really ask a tradesman to take care of an old chair when they are all busy with more urgent jobs. Meanwhile, my mother won't leave her alone. Without the chair, she's afraid she won't have any more visitors.

*The Role of God*

The few belongings people had are buried in rubble. The city is on its knees. Help isn't reaching certain parts of the population. For these people, what they hear on the radio—in other words, politics—doesn't concern them. They can count only on themselves. And God. They use God to convince themselves that they're not alone on this earth and that their lives are not just a beadwork of misery and pain. What matters most is their access to God at all times. They've understood that they can't ask too much of him. His spiritual resources may be infinite, but his material ones are limited. They lost their house, but they praise him for sparing their lives. I'm always surprised by what intellectuals say about the role of God among the poor. It has nothing to do with spirituality. It's like my mother's chair. It's better to have it in case a visitor shows up.

## A City of Art

If it's true that we have so many painters that we don't know what to do with them, we should give them a special place in the rebuilt city. A house is not just a shelter. And a city has to have a soul to be livable. What defines Port-au-Prince on the international scene? The brightly colored *tap-taps* that carry people from one place to another? Why not consider painting certain neighborhoods? Or turning Port-au-Prince into a city of art where music could play a role too? Haiti should use this truce to change its image. We won't have a chance like this a second time, if I can put it that way. Let's show a more relaxed face. Although everyone knows the reasons behind the tension (poverty, dictatorship, insecurity, hurricanes), it puts off visitors. Despite our troubles, our culture is joyful; we need to show it off. First, by separating art from craft. Haitian painting is a major art form. Why don't cities like Paris (Paris has done it more often than the others), New York, Rome, Montreal, Berlin, Tokyo, Madrid, Dakar, Abidjan, Sao Paulo, and Buenos Aires organize major exhibitions of Haitian art in their national museums? That would create interesting partnerships, and all sides would benefit. Haiti would recover its place among the nations. Its contribution would be artistic—and that's saying a lot.

*Brazil and Haiti*

Brazil has three things in common with Haiti: coffee, the love of soccer, and voodoo. They practice a variety of voodoo called *candomblé*. As for soccer, we hopped onto the Brazilian train a long time ago. Add to that the passion for music (the body fever of Carnival) and the rituals that come from Africa. We worship the Brazilian national soccer team to the point that we cheer for Brazil even when it plays against Haiti. I remember when Pelé came through Port-au-Prince. The city was literally transfixed.

I didn't go to the game, even if I did live close to the stadium. I was surprised to hear three loud cheers that shook the city. I went outside to find out what was going on. A guy was coming up the street, dancing with joy. I asked him how much Haiti was leading Brazil by. He looked at me like I was out of my mind and told me that Brazil had scored only three goals so far out of politeness for the host. In my memory, I can still hear him laughing all the way to the end of the street. At the beginning of the World Cup, every tent flew its Brazilian flag. The warm green and yellow colors made the city look happier somehow. The earthquake was no longer the first subject of conversation in this wounded place.

*Writer at Work*

When I came in, my nephew was writing on an old computer that he had put together himself. I sat down to watch him. I spotted a notebook close by in which he scribbled down something from time to time. Exactly the way I do. Yet I'd never told him anything about the way I work. Maybe he read it somewhere. Or maybe we have the same method. Writers at work all look the same. Suddenly, he turned to me.

"Are you writing?"

"I don't know …"

"I saw you."

"I wasn't writing."

We looked at each other a moment.

"Why do you refuse to accept that you were writing? That's what writers do."

"I'm not a writer," he stated in no uncertain terms.

"Why not?"

"I haven't written a book."

"A writer is just someone who writes."

He looked at me like a punch-drunk boxer. Now the issue of craft enters. A long road awaits him. He'll have to walk it by himself.


*A Sunday in Petit-Goâve*

I wanted to escape the uproar of Port-au-Prince, and the best time to cross the city of constant turmoil is early on a Sunday morning. I wanted to take that route again, but in an atmosphere different from Aunt Renée's funeral. See everything with a different point of view. From our house at Delmas 31 to the fragile shacks along the sea in Martissant, with fresh eyes I discovered a Port-au-Prince deep in slumber. I can't remember the last time I gazed upon the monster at rest. Even the gaudy *tap-taps*, those swift trucks that carry thousands of workers from the poor neighborhoods to the industrial zones, were hard to come by. A few party-goers were making their way home, crossing paths with elderly ladies going to early morning mass. Young girls with buckets of water on their heads. The district is overpopulated and very poor. All week, in the slums that have grown up around Port-au-Prince, there was only one subject in the air, and that was the unacceptable elimination of Brazil from the World Cup. People must have been emotionally exhausted (there were four deaths after Brazil's defeat). Once I got on the highway, I recovered that sense of exhilaration I always felt when I left Port-au-Prince for Petit-Goâve after year-end exams. On the road, I saw countless bicycles and little red-and-yellow motorbikes that serve as taxis, carrying girls who stared at me impassively, their expressions an obsession from my younger years. To the left, little houses with shutters painted yellow and blue like in the paintings they sell in front of the hotels. To the right, I glimpsed the sea, turquoise this time of day, behind the cane fields. Long stretches where you don't see anyone alternated with little markets, crowded even this early in the day. The sharp sunlight caught up with us at the foot of the terrible Tapion Mountain. Since childhood I've had this premonition that a truck will slide off the edge of the cliff with me in it. I got out to pick a mango and ate it beneath its tree—an old dream of mine. Then came Petit-Goâve, just on the other side of the mountain. I didn't recognize the entrance to the town. The new road doesn't go through the heart of town, which has grown in size. I've lost my bearings. I sorted through my memory—so rich in details when it comes to Petit-Goâve—but I couldn't locate any of these houses. The car turned right, toward the sea. And Petit-Goâve leaped up before my eyes. The same long, white, dusty street still crosses the town. We went past the hospital still standing with its back to the sea and continued to the little square by the marketplace. The new square is more handsome than the one from my childhood, but it doesn't have the same effect on me. I wish it were more natural, less prettied up. I wanted to see the port. That's where the adults would gather for an evening stroll when the July heat became unbearable. For teenagers, it was the perfect place for an innocent touch and an exchange of burning looks. When I think that's all it took to send me to seventh heaven. We went by the church, still clean and white; the religious songs and the noonday bells still live within me. From the church (that exists only in memory) to the elementary school where priests from Brittany looked after my education. The sisters' school, with its swarm of girls, reminded me of my years of thralldom to Vava. And Killick the teacher's house—he was the

happy too. My sister told me the neighbors were leeching off them. How's that? She went and rummaged through the drawers, then came back with a bundle of bills and shook them in my face. The figures were unbelievable. For months she's camped out in the electric company offices, the EDH, trying to get her bills lowered. She managed to speak to someone who understood the problem and who eliminated part of her debt, but on the next bill, the same amount showed up. It's enough to drive you crazy, she swore. My mother listened to the story from the doorway. These administrative irritations poison their lives. Everything here is designed to spoil your life, my sister declared. My mother said she has nothing left in her veins but poison. But they both agree they can't live without the little bit of electricity the EDH is willing to supply (four hours a day). Not only because it's useful, but because my sister refuses "to return to the Middle Ages." My mother agrees wearily; they've been engaged in this struggle forever. My sister, who almost never talks politics, said that the government treats poor people like animals. My mother agreed, but only to support her daughter.

## The Presidential Palace

We have started to miss our old lives. Life before January 12, 2010. To be exact, we enjoyed two-thirds of the day of January 12, since the earthquake occurred at 4:53 p.m. Up until 4:52, we lived carefree lives. We had one minute left. What is a minute worth? A lot, since the earthquake didn't even last a minute. The most shocking news was hearing that the Presidential Palace had collapsed. I remember the silence that followed the news. As if we had lost the war. Months later, we still can't get used to its absence. The place is the center point around which all dreams of grandeur and all the nation's hopes collide. Some people on the left are happy that the palace collapsed—for its symbolic value, I suppose. The poorest are the most saddened by its fall. They considered it the only house they could ever own; that idea is more deeply anchored in the ordinary citizen's mind than you might think. Every mother dreams that one day her first son will sit in the "presidential armchair." The fact that dictators have squatted there, more often than not over the past two hundred years, doesn't make that piece of furniture any less desirable. People have never mistaken the building for its occupier. One day they hope to restore its splendor. If a building's importance resides in the emotion its absence creates, then the palace has a value that's more than symbolic. A wave of feeling submerged the city, the whole country even, when we learned the palace had fallen with the first tremor. Now the Presidential Palace looks like an enormous white cake set on a low table of grass; it stirs envy and desire like a child on his birthday.

*January 11*

To help her with an article, on the day before the earthquake I went walking through the city with journalist Chantal Guy and photographer Ivanoh Demers. They came by the Hôtel Karibe early to get me. The sky was clear. Finally, the sun was shining. The week before the weather had been lousy, cloudy and cold. This was a piece about Port-au-Prince; they wanted to see the city through my eyes. The journalist was using me to get the editor-in-chief to accept an idea he'd already dismissed out of hand. They protested: "No, we want your view of the city. Your private Port-au-Prince is what we want to share with our readers." In that case, we'd have to go down to the Champ-de-Mars, the big square in front of the Presidential Palace. We went around the palace. I told them that under Papa Doc, we avoided going past the place. The surveillance was too heavy, and we didn't want to attract the attention of a *tonton-macoute* who happened to be in a bad mood. If we had to go by, we did it as quickly as possible and held our breath. Back then, the Champ-de-Mars was our destination. We went there to study and catch a breath of fresh air when it got too hot in our tin-roofed houses, play soccer with our pals, and chase the girls from the nearby neighborhoods who came to study for their exams too. Demers took pictures without bothering to frame the shots. He wanted to catch things on the fly. We headed for the little café (half a dozen tables) next to the Rex Theatre (the best hamburgers in town), and met the cashier I knew when I got a burger on Saturday nights after the western at the Rex. Across the way is the museum of the Collège Saint-Pierre where I first saw the works of Saint-Brice, Hector Hyppolite, Antonio Joseph, Cedor, Lazare, Philippe-Auguste, Wilson Bigaud, Rigaud Benoît, Jasmin Joseph—all the painters I discovered at the beginning of the 1970s. We walked along rue Capois, in front of the Lycée des Jeunes Filles, to rue Lafleur-Duchêne where I lived before I left Haiti for Montreal. I saw the house that I shared with my mother, my sister, and my aunts before they moved, once I'd left, for Carrefour-Feuilles, a humbler neighborhood, and more lively too. A lady invited me into her yard where she'd set up a hair salon underneath an awning. She was hoping to add a new room to her house before the year was out, since the clientele was getting larger by the day. Next to her, a woman getting her hair done made an off-color joke that I didn't quite catch, though it set off a wave of hilarity. When I left, she was still laughing. We continued down rue Capois to the Hôtel Oloffson where Graham Greene lived at the very beginning of the 1960s when he was writing *The Comedians*, the novel that, sadly enough, made Papa Doc famous. We sat down at a table and ordered a rum punch and waited for our plates of grilled conch. We all ordered the same thing, hoping that would speed up the service. The food is very good at the Oloffson, but you have to wait forever. We used the time to do a long interview and take a few extra photos. Then we returned to our respective hotels, with a date to meet the following day.

## A Word to the Gods

I wonder how long it will be before the event (an earthquake of magnitude seven) is taken up and transformed by voodoo. What do the gods have to say about it? Legba, where are you? Ogou, what do you have to say for yourself? Erzulie, what are your thoughts? Not a word. The gods are silent. If you're behind this thing, do you have some kind of a plan? What do you have in mind? What do you want? First, show yourselves.

## What Does Goudougoudou Want?

Can the popular imagination, which thrives on outsized events, inflate the unthinkable into something even greater? You can count on that. It just needs a little time. I wonder how the religions are going to use the earthquake's impact on people's minds. Every religion and denomination encumbering the Haitian landscape is furiously searching for the moment when it first predicted the earthquake. As January 12 turned into January 13, the Jehovah's Witnesses were already out in the streets of the ruined city, claiming that this was the end of the world as announced by Jehovah himself. Their day of glory had arrived. They'd been right to turn their backs on the world. Jehovah hadn't lied to them when he warned that God's wrath could shake the world at any time. He said he would come like a thief in the night and be as swift as lightning. And that's exactly what happened. The voodoo priests were more careful; they were abstaining from comment, at least for now. They didn't want to be held responsible for the disaster. The Protestants and Catholics had already pointed the finger at them. In their opinion, the devil was at work here. But if you ask me, the event will soon have its spot in the voodoo pantheon, and then we'll find out which god manifested his anger. Maybe the uproar is announcing the appearance of a new god. And that god already has a name in popular culture: "Goudougoudou," the sound the earth made as it trembled. Those who had no more faith in heaven watched the earth buckle beneath their feet. People were afraid of the hurricane's winds and the flood's waters, but the earth itself turned out to be a pitiless foe. What does Goudougoudou want?

*Time on TV*

Two kinds of time, if I can put it that way, face off in a fight to the death. One intends to eliminate the other: the time that belongs to nature and the time that belongs to television. In reality, the life of a people is counted in centuries, sometimes in millennia. When a society takes a new turn, sometimes we don't feel that breath of fresh air for another thirty years. The maceration occurs very slowly. Collective time is like that cow chewing its cud by the side of the road. Each car that whizzes past brings a new generation of new human beings with their particular sensibility, their own emotions and battles to fight. Our cow has seen so many cars rushing by that it doesn't even lift its head to look when a new one comes along. It will chew over the earthquake, and that will take the time it takes. The way it has only just finished chewing over the Duvalier era. That time is nearly immobile, and one man's death is no more than a blip on its screen. On the other hand, time on television is always accelerated. On TV, you can watch a rose bloom in ten seconds. In times of great turmoil, like now, people are glued to the small screen. Long enough for this artificial time to end up infiltrating their systems. When we watch television for too long, we start to think we can act upon events unfolding before our eyes. Everything in our lives seems too slow. We demand instant changes. Every time we come back from the bathroom, we want to see something new. We want progress. Why doesn't that truck go faster? We criticize people who are taking action, though we haven't moved from our armchair for the last two days. After a while, we figure it's time to move onto something else. If we can't change reality, we hope it will at least turn into fiction. That's what happens when we spend too much time watching television.

## A Visit to the Doctor

A little cat at my mother's feet with eyes so soft, almost frightened, you'd think it was a mouse. We found it in the yard after the earthquake. My mother adopted it immediately, and ever since they've been whispering secrets to each other. And understanding everything, according to my sister. My mother has left the gallery, and the little cat watches her go, completely at a loss, as if its world has just collapsed. We're waiting for my mother in the car. My sister is taking her to the doctor's, something she detests above all things. She looks exactly like the little cat. She comes out of the house, then returns to look for something, but won't tell us what it was. She's really just stalling. My sister wants to be the first in line at the clinic, since she has only the morning off. If the appointment doesn't take too long, we'll have time to get to the lab and do the tests before eleven o'clock. Then she'll drop us back at the house and rush off to work. She's already starting to sweat. She's done everything at top speed this morning: making breakfast at the house and planning the day's meal with the cook. She has so many things to sort out (the bills, for starters) as she looks after my mother, who has developed all sorts of capricious manners; her son, who never has what he needs for school; her husband, who catches a new disease every morning; her daughter overseas, who's depressed—no wonder she doesn't have time to think about post-earthquake stress disorder, which is the theme this week on the radio. Ever since some psychiatrists got on TV and declared that Haiti is an excellent laboratory for studying post-earthquake stress disorder, that spice is being added to every sauce. Everything is seen from that angle. You get to work late. That's due to post-earthquake stress disorder, even if you've never been on time in your life. Finally, my mother gets into the car and we drive off. My nephew left with his father. My sister figures they have a fifty-fifty chance of getting a flat tire on the way, which makes my mother burst out laughing. My sister tells me the doctor is good, but a little expensive. We get there, wait a short time, then we're ushered into his office. A large, restful room. The doctor is a thin man, concerned with his own appearance, but he seems competent; in any case he has a dry manner with the discreet warmth of efficient people. My mother is always intimidated when there's a doctor around. My sister is attentive and care-worn. The doctor, half-serious and half-jovial, looks a little worried at the sight of my mother's swollen foot, especially the wound on her right leg. He scribbles a few instructions on a pad and sends us off to get tests. The results will be expedited to a specialist. In the car, I say that the doctor is lucky that his clinic escaped undamaged. My sister tells me he's been kidnapped at least twice. He's a brave man. That's the minimum you can expect when you live here, my sister says, staring straight ahead. We went to have the tests done at a private laboratory, so we won't have to wait so long. I expected to see people with a certain income level there, but they come from everywhere. They weren't talking about the earthquake—only the difficulty of keeping their heads above water. Finally, they called my mother's name. Her anxiety was visible even in the nape of her neck. I'd forgotten how frail she is. She lists to one side, and her little black purse keeps slipping off her shoulder. Her face is radiant when she returns; she didn't have to have a shot. We drove straight home, and my sister went off to work.

## New Art Forms

What art form will be the first to come forward after the earthquake? Poetry, so impulsive, or painting, eager for new landscapes? Where will the first images of the earthquake be seen? On the city walls or the bodies of *tap-taps*? Will the short story, not as fast as poetry but quicker than the novel, come back into fashion? The novel demands a minimum of comfort that Port-au-Prince can't offer; it's an art form that flourishes in industrialized nations. Are writers already at work? Will we see a race to write the great earthquake novel or the major essay about reconstruction? And the winner—will it be Frankétienne or a young, unknown woman novelist? Dalembert or a German writer who'd never even heard of Haiti before the event? Don't forget that the great novel of the Haitian dictatorship (*The Comedians*, 1966) was written by Graham Greene, an Englishman. The earthquake is a planetary event. It belongs to everyone. What would we think if this great tragic novel ended up being written by a talented, yet mannered, young upper-class writer? Would we take that book for what it is (a masterpiece) or see it as the ultimate slap from a jesting god? What style would it be written in? Ironic or tragic? Could it be comic, even if so many people died? Laughter to tears? Who will censor the works that don't live up to the standard of what is tolerable? The church, the state, or society? Do artists who weren't present at the time have the necessary legitimacy to turn the earthquake into a work of art? Is the new Haitian someone who went through the event? The race has begun. But we've lost something: our intimacy. Everyone is carefully scrutinized now. Just to speak your mind, you have to show you're clean. Say how many deaths you had in your family. As if it were a war, not an earthquake. When it comes to the Lisbon earthquake, Voltaire's poem is what remains.

## Social Bonds

There are hundreds, perhaps thousands of teenagers orphaned by the earthquake. Some have lost all their family members. If we allow them to drift, it won't take long before we have a serious crime problem in this country. People think twice about killing when they have relationships with others. When the opposite is true, they develop a terrifying insensitivity. They'd hesitate to rob a woman who happens to be the mother of a schoolmate. Or kill a former teammate for his money. These bonds develop during childhood. They make us an integral part of society, and we owe it something. If we don't start working on the social network, the city will soon become fragmented and gangs will multiply.

## A Faithful Friend

I met Marcus for the first time in 1972 at a talk at the Institut français. I had just finished secondary school and had registered in the ethnology department, which, in my hopeful opinion, was one of the rare spots in Port-au-Prince where you could catch a good nap while getting an education. It was the final refuge for people who had failed to enter a more prestigious department, like medicine, engineering, or agronomy. Law wasn't worth much at the time, but it was more highly rated than ethnology. The latter is useful in Haiti, but only if you want to do research on voodoo, traditional music, and sacred dances. You had to wear a full beard, a peasant shirt, and a few necklaces of dried *maldioc* beans. I whiled away the afternoons at the university, not far from the Palace movie theater, discussing Dr Price-Mars' theories on the influence of African culture on Haitian identity, and the impact of French culture, which meant Parisian, on the local bourgeoisie. One evening, I met up with Marcus again at a show at the Collège Saint-Pierre museum, and he asked me to come and work with him at the Haïti-Inter radio station. I was a reporter for the midday news show that he was directing. Since we were neighbors, he on ruelle Roy and I on Lafleur-Duchêne, we used to have breakfast together. His wife Jocelyne wasted no time adopting me. We listened to Wagner, since Marcus had developed an addiction to his music during an internship in France. Every morning we'd go jogging in the Champ-de-Mars, discussing the political situation, or more often than not the complicated relation between power and the press. We had to watch what we said. There were signs that government spies had infiltrated the media, passing themselves off as independent journalists. Which was why we did our talking as we ran around the edge of the park.

Marcus was a very meticulous journalist who hated rumors. He insisted on backing up every statement with facts, in a country where everyone was forever making up stories. The government, the opposition, the press, people in their daily lives, everyone was busy inventing a private universe that had no relation to reality. I wondered how he had developed his passion for fact. I saw him lose his head only once: the day his daughter was born. He came by the house because he wanted me to go to the hospital with him. The effort to maintain his self-control made him seem more wound up. I pretended I didn't notice anything. He drove around the Presidential Palace three times in a row. Normally we avoided the place. It was infested with the regime's henchmen, and a flat tire could have disastrous results. We reached the hospital untouched. His happiness was something to see when he learned he had a daughter. Yet he waited a month before he took the baby in his arms. His wife Jocelyne would give me desperate looks until one morning, just before getting into his car to drive to the radio station, he turned to her and took the baby. You should have seen her ecstatic look! Marcus was the first to tell me about the death of Gasner Raymond, the friend who shared a byline with me at *Le Petit Samedi Soir*, a weekly that covered politics and culture, and that was barely tolerated by the government. I left for Montreal after Gasner was murdered in June of 1976, and in November 1980, Marcus was thrown in prison with all the other independent journalists who called for elections in the country, since the Duvalier regime had been in power since 1957. Later, the group was sent into exile. We met again in New York. There was a return to Haiti in 1986 after Jean-Claude Duvalier left. We lost track of each other then, but came together again in Miami in 1990 when I moved there from Montreal to have a quieter place to write. I lived in Kendall, in the southwest, and he was next to Little Haiti. Every time I went to see my aunts there, I'd stop by and spend some time with Marcus and Jocelyne. He was still active and publishing a political weekly, *Haïti-Demain*, and hosting a radio show. We discussed all kinds of things, jumping from politics to literature, not to mention the gossip of everyday life. We also talked a lot about American culture, which fascinated both of us, even if we did live in the belly of the beast. I would bring escapist novels for Jocelyne who was still nostalgic about life in Port-au-Prince. She went back as soon as she got the chance. It was more difficult for Marcus; he had to stay in Miami for his newspaper and his radio show. His dream was to have a station in Haiti. With his friend Lucien Andrews, he did just that, years later. It became Mélodie FM. That's where I met him today, at noon. He entrusted me to his young team of reporters as he finished the next issue of *Haïti-Demain*. I looked around the station and felt I'd traveled back in time to the mid-1970s. Then Batraville showed up, and we talked for a while (they served us coffee) in Marcus's office, though he hadn't finished the issue yet. Nothing could distract him from his work, even a friend he hadn't seen in more than ten years. We got around to talking about what Marcus was able to save from the ruins of his house after the earthquake. He described everything in a neutral tone, without pathos. I know him well: he'd throw himself into a raging river to rescue a dog. He was at the station when it happened. As soon as he understood it was an earthquake, he went home. He knew Jocelyne was dead when he saw the empty space where his house had been. She had to be in there. At that time of day, she would have been knitting in front of the TV. And it was true: he found her underneath a beam. He rushed her to the hospital but it was too late. He carried her body to a friend's house before going back to the station. Why go back? Mélodie FM, he told me, a small station, was the only one on the air that night, along with Signal FM. "I'm a journalist. I couldn't miss a scoop like that," he said in a steady voice. It was only the second time in the country's history that a major earthquake had hit Port-au-Prince (we didn't know yet that Léogâne, Petit-Goâve, and Jacmel were affected too). He stayed and helped inform people about how the situation was developing, and he didn't leave the studio for days. I imagined Marcus that way. His wife's body was safe, so he returned to work. One-hundred-percent professional. When I left, he gave me a little radio for my mother. She was so too much attention will end up suffocating the patient. Except, of course, if your profession makes you useful on the ground. We've all witnessed that comic scene in which one person is doing all the work while a crowd mills around him. You're never far from a television camera in Port-au-Prince, now that the city has been turned into a giant set. In this new invasion of Haiti (everyone wants to be at the bedside of the celebrated patient), a lot of organizations and people are in it for their own personal visibility. Of course, a good number of organizations and individuals are completely sincere. How can we separate the wheat from the chaff? No need to waste time with that. As soon as the cameras pull out, the sorting will begin immediately. No sense pushing and shoving; if you want to help, you'll find a way. I know someone who left Montreal and returned to Port-au-Prince right after the earthquake. Guided only by emotion. Today, he is among the ranks of people who depend on international aid to survive. The country needs energy, not tears.

## The Local Market

I'm surprised when my sister brings home refrigerated vegetables from the supermarket when there are such good fresh ones at a better price from the local market. My sister is obsessed with germs—that's the problem. The market is teeming with them, or so she imagines, while supermarket vegetables are kept far from the flies and dust behind their envelope of cellophane. But since the earthquake and the collapse of the Caribbean Market, everyone knows it's risky to enter the supermarkets that weren't built according to earthquake standards, whereas there's no risk at all in an outdoor market. After the first week, everyone carefully avoided any covered structures. But in no time, those who had a certain level of buying power, since prices went up instead of falling, started flocking back to the supermarkets. Every neighborhood is defined by its supermarket. If you don't see one near you, it's because you're not in the right part of town. For us, it's the Eagle Market. Since the Caribbean Market collapsed, the neighborhood stores have recovered some of their customers. Even the little outdoor market, where the vegetables are laid out on a jute sack on the ground, shared in the influx of buyers. We go there in the evening, just before the vendors start putting away their produce, to get the best prices. Everyone bargains hard at that market, while in the supermarket, they are happy to pay the price on the package, no questions asked. The customers obey the strong and crush the weak and hope to balance their budget that way. It's very important not to be seen by a co-worker from the office when you go to the outdoor market where the flies land gaily on the meat (don't forget to boil it hard). The technique is simple: you stay in your car until you've spotted the product you want. When there aren't many people around, usually just before nightfall, when the women start bundling up their vegetables, you spring from your car and pounce on that sack of yams you've had your eye on for the last hour. Often you're not the only one who has spotted a good deal. Sometimes you find yourself face-to-face with the one person you were hoping not to meet. In that case, you'll have to share that sack of yams. My sister told me that story. Ever since, she and the woman have been going to the market together.

## The Debate

We shouldn't leave things (and here I mean the apocalyptic decor) too long in the state they're in. People will end up getting used to it, and they will stop being surprised by what they see. Some will want to live in the safer part of a ruined house if they're sure there won't be any more tremors. Plants will start growing here and there, and life will pick up where it left off. The strength that helped the population overcome great misfortune can lead it to accept anything. Those people who revealed themselves to be exceptional in the most difficult times can be quite awkward in ordinary life. Sometimes we need to leave room for those who are able to take charge of organizing daily life without getting bogged down in ideological discourse. Leave the way free for people who have a sense of ordinary time and who refuse to remain on the alert constantly. It's better to make plans when you're not being pushed and pulled every which way. After a great period of excitement that makes you feel you're experiencing something unique every day, now we need people whose lamps stay lit all through the night. They're working to design the world in which we will live. That's not always a good thing. What isn't? Leaving your future in the hands of total strangers. We got used to being the planet's center of attention too quickly. Where are the cameras now? Elsewhere, for there are other nations who have been waiting to warm themselves by that artificial fire.

*I Was There*

I know a man in New York who so much wanted to be in Haiti at the time of the earthquake that he started telling everyone he was there. Finally, he admitted that he was actually in Florida. Strangely, he was ashamed not to have been there as the shadow of death lay across the country. He even imagined himself buried in the ruins. Do we need to remind him that those who died desired only to live? They don't want his presence at their side. They'd prefer it if he remained in the world of the living. You don't become Haitian by dying. Another man I met in Tallahassee would have liked to have been in Port-au-Prince for historical reasons. He believed something important happened there. The breath of history. And he missed it. A historical moment that, in his personal mythology, was as major as January 1, 1804. A founding moment that should produce a new Haitian discourse. People are going to examine that issue from every angle in the decades to come. Politicians, intellectuals, and demagogues won't miss an opportunity to drop an "I was there" into the conversation. But being there did not make a better citizen out of anyone. Some guy who had always lived overseas and who happened to be in Port-au-Prince that afternoon will escape that horrible label of "diaspora"; suddenly he will achieve nobility. He becomes an "I was there." Whereas someone who always lived in Haiti and wasn't in the country that day will lose a little of his national luster. He might even be outdistanced by the traveler from another country who barely escaped death. These days, more than life, death defines our sense of belonging.

*The Tire*

The "little mechanic" (little because he's poor) came to fix my brother-in-law's car this morning at 6:30. He's a frequent visitor because my brother-in-law, like many citizens of Port-au-Prince, has a passionate relationship with his mechanic. They see each other at least once a week—two or three times a day during a crisis. I have a friend who leaves his car with his mechanic and takes it back only when he really needs it—his way of paying him. My brother-in-law doesn't go that far. Their relationship is based on tires. A good tire (forget your criteria) can last at least a week. A bad one, not even a day. Before the earthquake, the "little mechanic" (actually, he's tall and thin) came by every morning to inspect the tire. Any number of times, my sister, who has a practical side, offered to pay for a new tire with her own money (often it's the right front wheel) just so she wouldn't have to see the "little mechanic" every morning, but my brother-in-law, who treasures this ritual as much as his *Nouvelliste* every evening or his morning cup of coffee, always turned down my sister's offer. Sitting on the gallery, every morning I am treated to the same scene. There's a knock at the gate. My brother-in-law goes to open it. The "little mechanic" enters. They make small talk about the intensity level of things in the public sphere—in other words, my brother-in-law wants to know if there was gunfire last night in the poorer parts of town. Then they move on to more serious issues: a meticulous inspection of the air pressure of the four tires. The "little mechanic" carefully examines each tire, then lingers on the right front. Will it survive the day? The answer is often negative, but hope springs eternal. My brother-in-law asks him to proceed, then goes back to the dining room for a second cup of coffee. This morning, it took longer than usual. The "little mechanic" was happy to find everyone safe and sound, and the house still habitable. The wall collapsed, but the "little mechanic" thinks his brother can fix it today. My brother-in-law figured it was a good deal, but just as he was about to agree to the terms, we heard an awful scream from deep inside the house. My sister's cry of protest: she would not accept seeing the mechanic and his stone-mason brother every morning for the rest of her life. The "little mechanic" burst out laughing. Even my brother-in-law managed a smile. The deal was postponed. For

*The Panic*

My mother is slowly getting over the inflammation in her leg. Her heart rate is more normal. Her appetite is returning. She's lost that listless mood that made me so afraid. The last time we sat together in her room, she spoke of her own death. Not directly— that's not like her. In a soft voice, she warned that she couldn't wait for me very much longer. She has spent her life waiting for my return. She lowered her head as she spoke then smiled up so discreetly that you'd have to be watching for it. She's decided to return to church the next Sunday. She's eager to see that handicapped man who, my sister told me, is the only person who really depends on my mother. Although she's frail and ill, she knows she's in better condition than that man. Slumped in front of the church day and night, he scarcely raises his eyes when people give him alms. But when he sees my mother, his body moves in her direction, and he tries to lift himself from his chair. His frenetic dance (with drooling and dissonant gestures) frightens some of the faithful, but the joy that shines on his face makes my mother happy. She needs that bond, especially since she is beginning to depend on others. She is facing the unknown valiantly, but I see the panic in her eyes.

## Madness

Mental health problems are the lowest on the list of current illnesses. Madness is not considered a sickness, but the result of cruel destiny. It's a consolation to know that in poor countries, the insane are not excluded. They fulfill their function as madmen with the right to act mad. In richer countries, where they receive special care, the mad are segregated. They have no social function. They are objects of shame and are hidden away. They disappear from circulation, often from one day to the next. Only to reappear once they have shown the ability to imitate the rest of society. In Haiti, people make cruel mockery of your anxieties. Sometimes that shock treatment is beneficial. Those who can't stay on track are pushed to the side, and the crowd moves on. The word "trauma" has been heard lately from the mouths of international specialists describing the earthquake survivors. Of course this kind of situation calls for attention and care, but will people be willing to accept help? It's difficult to treat an illness denied by the population and the person most concerned. The only thing recognized as discomfort here is merciless pain that refuses to abate after three days.

## Laughter and Death

You have to talk about it in the coarsest of ways, using vulgar words. The way people still do at gatherings in the countryside. Baron Samedi's exaggeratedly sexual dance begins the festivities on the Day of the Dead. The extreme carnival of the *guédés* (voodoo spirits), who pour alcohol and vinegar into their mouths as they crunch on broken bottles adds to the atmosphere. Sex is the energy closest to death. In the Middle Ages, the orgasm was called *la petite mort*. This stuff isn't made for parlors and powdered cheeks. Poets don't do very well with it, except for Villon, who pleads for pity for the hanged men twisting in agony, left along the side of the road, at the mercy of the elements. Men have never domesticated death. It has always been tribal, ordinary, and obscene. Death is the origin of life, not the other way around.

## A New City

People have the right to say what kind of city they want to live in. Even better, they should be able to get involved in drawing up the plans. That being said, they might admit they don't have the necessary talent. And while they're at it, understand as well that they won't be alone on this new ground: eight million individuals have the same rights they do. The work site could end up absorbing the energy of several generations of men and women of all social strata. We shouldn't lose sight of the fact that the real inhabitants of the new city have not yet been born. I mean those who will know the former city only through old photographs, since things will have changed considerably in thirty or forty years. Building a city is a much more ambitious project than a bridge or a skyscraper. On the purely technical level, it takes knowledge that demands the participation of several trades. The most important material is the spirit. A spirit open to the world, not concentrated on itself. Let's abandon the insular mentality that keeps us in warm, sterile self-satisfaction. A new city that will compel us to enter a new life. That's what will take time. Time we haven't given ourselves.

*A Reunion*

I came to Port-au-Prince for secondary school, after a childhood watched over by my grandmother in a small provincial town.

Port-au-Prince was an enormous city, and my mother, my sister, and my aunts were the only people I knew. We all lived together on avenue Bouzon, near the cemetery. We lived near the Sylvio Cator Stadium, where the national soccer championships took place, and close to the Salomon market, the Montparnasse movie theater, and place Saint-Alexandre which, years later, would become place Carl Brouard in honor of the anarchist poet. The neighborhood was lively, and it both attracted and frightened me. My arrival would change the rhythm of the house. My mother and my aunts were women of calm and reserved manner (except Aunt Raymonde, who had a melodramatic streak) and my sister an obedient adolescent who spent most of her time at the house helping my mother with the housework. My mother carefully selected the people we were allowed to associate with. Among the rare acceptable families were the Preptits. The father was a former military officer put under house arrest by Papa Doc, which forced him inside for years. The only time you saw him on the street was late in the evening. The mother was a discreet, refined woman who tended toward sadness. You felt that they had once been a brilliant, worldly couple (a painting of the young officer and his wife in the living room spoke of carefree happiness) who were invited out everywhere. Then suddenly the void swallowed them up. For me, all that was very mysterious. It took me a long time to realize the disgrace was political. The energy of the five Preptit children kept the house from sinking into depression. My friend Claude (the eldest) was so serious he even played seriously. But when he did laugh, you could feel the happy child whose sense of responsibility, thrust upon him too early, had made him solemn. I was more the dreamy type. We played ping-pong on Saturday mornings. His father built us a rudimentary table. In the summer, we organized a local badminton championship in the big yard next door. The taste for games was rare in Haiti, and it came from his father who had played them at the military academy. We kept up our friendship until I left the neighborhood. We lost track of each other when I changed schools. A few years later, I left Haiti, but Claude stayed on. In Montreal I heard that he'd become a very good engineer; the trade fit him like a glove. Later, when I was at a literary festival in Port-au-Prince (*Livres en folie*), Claude came up to the table where I was sitting. People had been talking a lot about him for the last months, and the reason was obvious: he was an engineer, and he'd been predicting a major earthquake in Haiti for years. Preptit stated that Port-au-Prince would be the hardest hit. His knowledgeable manner and serious tone made you listen. His predictions frightened people in a country never short on disasters: floods, hurricanes, dictatorship. But in Haiti, if you're frightened one minute, you're dancing the next. This tried-and-true method keeps people from sinking into collective depression. In our society, it's better to be diverse and changeable.

And not take a blind alley all alone. Preptit stuck with his predictions, though people thought he was exaggerating. They started whispering about the state of his mental health. When invited to speak in the media, his answers never varied.

A brief dialogue between him and a journalist (imaginary, but based on information gathered from various sources):

> Q: When will it happen?
> A: The earthquake could occur at any time.
> Q: Could you be more precise?
> A: Now, or in ten years.
> Q: Now?
> A: Yes. Even as we are speaking.
> Q: And what are the possible risks?
> A: Difficult to evaluate, but everything indicates enormous proportions.
> Q: Thousands of deaths?
> A: Possibly, perhaps more.

His academic tone made people nervous. They were fascinated by this man, who calmly announced the coming apocalypse. In the street, they stopped to question him. Why didn't he leave if he was so sure what was going to happen? He wasn't the kind of man who would abandon his city. I recognized my friend from avenue Bouzon. The son of a military man. You don't leave a sinking ship. I looked up and greeted him. We smiled. He had wanted to see me again. Silence between us. How was it for you? He told me he was in the yard when it happened. He knew it was at least a magnitude seven. Here was the event he'd been predicting for ten years. What did you think at the time? "Honestly, it was a relief. It was the proof that I wasn't crazy." I saw a lost look in his eyes. He'd done everything to warn the population, but no one had listened. Instead, they mocked him. Now that it's too late, everyone is consulting him. The people in line started getting impatient. He shook my hand, gave me a sad smile that reminded me of my mother, then disappeared into the crowd.


*Secret Ceremony*


Now that foreigners are finding their way to Haiti, they'll be sure to fall under the spell of voodoo again. Volunteers (all those former religious types who have recycled themselves into humanitarian workers) and intellectuals are going to simmer in the old colonial kettle. Instead of wasting precious time chasing after fake voodoo ceremonies, they would be better off trying to understand the nation by seriously studying its vision of the world. The first man who says, "I attended a secret ceremony" should be laughed out of the country. If it really was secret, you wouldn't be accepted. Why was your presence tolerated at a secret ceremony? For money? You're quick to answer the question: "No, I didn't pay." Which had you concluding it was a real ceremony. In any case, either you paid in advance without realizing it (the ceremony organized for your benefit was a reward for your past good deeds), or you'll pay later. One way or another. There are so many rules you can't know in this universe heavy with false mysteries. If you're there, the ceremony isn't secret. Remember the old saying: if someone else knows, it's not a secret.

*Ancient Knowledge*

These people who bear their pain with extraordinary grace have such a sense of life, and it would be a shame to ignore it. Seeing their serenity, you can imagine how much they know about pain, hunger, and death, and how much violent joy lives inside them.

Joy and pain are transformed in singing and in dance. What can we do with such knowledge? We sometimes see it shining through in the colorful canvases of the naïve painters or in that irresistible music that loses itself in its own explosive joy. If we listen more carefully, we might be surprised to discover that the words that got us up on the dance floor are achingly sad. That's where the secret of this country resides. And not in the ready-made voodoo served up to tourists and Haitians who have been out of the country too long.

## The Energy of Money

We know about the energy that money brings. It's an aggressive force that happily sweeps aside everything in its path. The man who helps you sometimes grants himself the privilege of judging you. The least you can do is listen to him. The argument runs like this: your knowledge has failed. Don't bother protesting, because that's the truth. He's helping you, and not the other way around. He'll shove his culture in your face with a tone of false humility, which is the worst vanity of all, along with the arrogance that comes from believing that the other guy hasn't understood the situation—and that he's swallowed your line whole. Those who have come to help should receive a crash course in popular culture: if someone listens to you without interrupting, it's not because you're interesting, it's because the other guy is waiting for you to finish so he can get down to serious business: money. Do you have any? And how much? In small bills, if possible. I've heard the directors of big companies and humanitarian organizations state in no uncertain terms for the camera that they're here to help people, and have no ulterior motives. That's possible. But why do they get angry when the other guy forgets to kneel down and thank them? The problem is that, over time, Third-World populations have developed a welfare mentality. They know the workings of the international aid system—we can sense that. They have studied it carefully. Some of them have nothing else to do. They know that the amounts distributed by private individuals are reimbursed by the tax departments and ministries of revenue in their home countries. The money has its source in the workings of accountants. Then you have to factor in the aura of belonging to a group of people with a social conscience. The information circulating among the poor has given them the impression that they are partners, not dependents. Which saddens those people whose job it is to help, and who are only asking for a little recognition in return. But the clever folks in the Fourth World have quickly understood that recognition has an exchange value and shouldn't

She held my hand. Her eyes were on mine. I felt her gentleness.

"I'm not going to claim I sent money to Haiti. I don't have enough for that. But I've prayed a lot for the Haitian people. Proud, clean people who don't deserve such a fate … I wonder how they get along."

"They do everything possible to live as long as possible."

"I understand … I have nothing to give, like I told you. Except my heart."

"That's a lot, madame. Your gift will be delivered. I'll see to it myself."

She took me in her arms again.

*Calvary Mountain*

Our cook lives on Calvary Mountain. To return home after work, she has to walk a good twenty minutes to get out of Delmas 31 where our house is, then she waits for a *tap-tap* on the highway that will take her to Pétionville, in front of place Saint-Pierre, and from the square, she walks the rest of the way. On rainy days, like today, my sister drives her home. Instead of staying inside and watching the rain fall, I go with them. The city is under water. The wind is at gale force. The vendors we drive by are soaked to the skin. They climb the slope, their eyes closed against the pelting rain that punishes their faces. We reach Calvary Mountain. This is the first time that I've come up here. I get a sick feeling every time I come close to the cliff. I've always associated this region with the ladies who sell us those fat onions and juicy carrots that smell of the rich earth. In fact, this is the richest zone in Haiti— unless there's one richer that I don't know about. I've never seen so many magnificent villas. Giant pine trees surround them or stand on either side of the entryways like faithful sentinels. A feeling of peacefulness holds sway here; it makes you want to die. You have to keep reminding yourself that you're not on the shores of Lake Geneva. I'm not envious, actually, and I don't care about other people's wealth. I haven't internalized the class struggle, but here I'm really astounded. And to think my cook lives next to such abundance. Every day she walks through this district and goes down to work in the heart of Delmas. And never a complaint. She thinks that's as normal as the rain pelting the roof of the car. Most of these houses are empty. Their owners spend part of the year in Italy and part in England or somewhere else. I'm not criticizing their lifestyle (I travel a lot myself), but the fruit rotting on the ground and the empty rooms are a shame in a city where the majority of the population lives in precarious conditions. On the way back down, we go past the camp on place Saint-Pierre.

When you think that the people who live here get hit with a downpour almost every evening and that the wind sometimes blows away their tents. And that every morning luxury automobiles from Calvary Mountain (a calvary for whom?) rush past them, driving children to school. I wonder if those children ever ask their parents about how the other children (it's the same word for both groups) live, the ones they see emerging, fully dressed, from that anthill. Maybe no one sees what's so obvious. But I'm sure that kids pick up on the situation right away. It's not surprising that some leave home as soon as they can. Some kinds of pain can't be silenced with drugs.

*Living Together*

I wonder what happens in those tents that have sprung up everywhere. How do people manage to preserve their private lives? Do men who snore too loud have to sleep during the day to keep from waking everyone up at night? People are experiencing a dual misfortune: individual (they have lost friends and family) and collective (they have lost their city). How do they find a way to mourn their dead when it's so difficult to get a moment to yourself? It's easy to imagine idyllic scenes under starry skies, but where do people actually make love? In thickets, where cries of pleasure won't be heard. They say that in some camps, there's an empty tent with a sign that says "For the moment." A way of having a sweet interlude in a discreet setting. We know that neither fear nor pain nor indigence will keep desire from flowering. It doesn't take very much: the bend of a neck, eyes that linger—and everything changes. It's the only thing that can get our minds off a difficult situation. And how is food shared with new neighbors? Does family hierarchy continue in a tent city? Living in a group requires constant discretion if you don't want to offend other people. The poorest are ahead in this game, since they're used to rubbing elbows; they're not afraid of touching each other. Some individuals feel physical revulsion at the idea of rubbing up against people they consider lower class. It's possible that an unexpected situation, if it lasts long enough, will cause major changes in people's lives.

*Reading in a Tent*

For adults, it's desire. For kids, reading. A child lost in *The Three*

*Musketeers* isn't living in a tent. He's in a Dumas novel. A life of adventure. Galloping through the night. When he gets tired, he stops at an inn and wakes the innkeeper, who was sleeping next to the missus in his nightcap. He sits down before a copious meal after ordering a bale of hay for his horse, which has been sent to the stables. It is no easy task, for the roads are not safe. Suddenly, he is surrounded by a group of masked riders. Just as d'Artagnan is about to unsheathe his sword, he hears a voice that is too familiar and too shrill to be Milady's. It's the young reader's mother calling him for supper. She smiles when she sees her son come running with a book under his arm.

## The Prodigal Son

I went back to the Hôtel Karibe, where it all began. The feeling of returning to the scene: one foot in the past (that vibration again) and the other in the present. Which has me shaking a little. I didn't go through the front door for fear the return would be too sudden. I chose the side entrance, the exact spot where I met Saint-Éloi who had just arrived on that January 12, about 3:30 pm. The conference room wasn't too badly damaged. I went through the courtyard. The rear façade of the hotel has been repaired. I stepped onto the tennis courts where shadows once moved. The swimming pool, its surface unmoving. The garden with its flowers that withstood the earthquake. In the restaurant, I came upon the owner who hugged me passionately. When I congratulated him for not having lost his cool during those difficult days, and most of all for having stayed with his guests when he could have gone home to sleep, he told me confidentially, "Instead of destroying me, the tragedy gave me the energy I needed to do better." Just then the waiter appeared, the same one who was serving us just before the earthquake. The plump man was wearing the same warm smile he'd never lost, even at the worst times of the crisis. I reminded him I was still waiting for a lobster, and that he had gone to get it when the earthquake struck. He gave me a sly smile, then disappeared into the kitchen. I was talking with a chambermaid when he returned bearing a lobster. So fast? He'd wanted to surprise me and sent the order as soon as he saw me come through the gate. We laughed. I was moved. I sat down at the table where I'd been on January 12, when disaster visited us, and this time I was able to enjoy my lobster in peace.

*The Tenderness of the World*

Wherever I go, people speak in low voices. Their conversations are cut with silence. Eyes averted, they reach for my hand. Through me, they hope to speak to the island that has been wounded, but has escaped its isolation. People ask me for news. They quickly realize they are better informed than I am. I removed myself from that poisonous buzzing, better to preserve the images that burn inside me. On the first night, that little girl who was worried if there would be school the next day. Or the mango lady the following morning, sitting on the ground, back against a wall, with her pile of mangos for sale. When people speak to me, I see in their eyes that they are addressing the dead, while I am clinging to the slightest crumb of life. But what really touches me is how moved they seem by their own emotion and how they hope to keep it with them as long as possible. They say one catastrophe replaces another. Journalists can go prospecting elsewhere, but Haiti will continue to occupy the heart of the world for a long time to come.

The way this book forced itself on me is really no surprise. On the tennis court, I made up my mind not to let the earthquake upset my schedule. Not that I'm insensitive to what happened. When I close my eyes, the images come rushing back in all their horror. The only way I can breathe is to move. I owed my publisher Rodney St-Éloi a book. It was supposed to be notes about writing. On my previous visit to Port-au-Prince, my nephew wouldn't stop bugging me with all his questions about style. I refused to answer; the issue is bound up with the act of writing itself. Which is like saying you learn to write by writing. Good writers are their own masters. The main thing is to be attentive to two fundamental points: music and rhythm. If you have a tin ear, you might as well do something else. No one can teach you how to write a sentence that sounds good. My nephew kept insisting. He was looking for specific advice. "And not another book that's going to make me feel desperate," he called on his way to the bathroom. I ended up accepting the challenge. The title was ready-made: *Notes to a Young Writer in Pajamas*. I know it might sound pretentious to start giving advice. But I figured that over the last thirty-five years, I must have learned a thing or two about writing that I could tell him. Like keeping the spontaneity that adds so much charm. Everything seems much too clean these days (now the old man is judging his contemporaries). Buffon was right when he said that style *is* the man. I like to feel there's someone behind the door. Even if you have talent, you can't make it without character. The book (*Notes to a Young Writer in Pajamas*) was finished, but it still required careful rereading. I needed time to write. I had two weeks to make the necessary corrections. Don't go thinking that those two weeks were waiting for me with a smile. Every day was filled with something else. I've understood for some time now that I can have whatever I want—except time. André Breton was a prospector for the gold of time. I don't have it. Don't have it any more. The freer I feel in my mind, the less I belong to myself. Freedom gives off a scent that attracts people. I looked at my calendar. Three trips in the month of March. I had two weeks before the book was due at the publisher's. I threw my notebook and my little Toshiba computer into my suitcase.

*Tallahassee Hotel*

Last year, Martin Monroe, a professor and specialist in Caribbean literature, invited me to a colloquium on contemporary Haitian literature. I couldn't really refuse since I had just gotten through declaring in Port-au-Prince that culture was the only thing Haiti had produced in the last two hundred years. Culture is the only thing that can stand up to the earthquake. I'm not only talking about intellectual culture, the kind that comes from books, but what structures a nation. If we don't want to turn into a victim nation, we have to keep moving. We'll cry later when things are better. In the meantime, let's go forward. That was my decision. The hotel wasn't far (a twenty-minute walk) from Florida State University where my eldest daughter studied French-language literature. Why an American university? "American schools are loaded with money," she told me at the time. "They can line up three Nobel Prize winners at the same table." Really? This big conference about Haiti had been in the works for two years. It was my first contact with a university since my return. I decided to add a short text about the earthquake at the end of my book about style. I would relate my first impressions when the tremors struck. That turned out to be my Pandora's box. Gold fever. Every time I had a free moment, I slipped back to my room. If I had one piece of advice for a young writer, it would be this: "Write about what makes you passionate. Don't look for the subject; the subject will find you." Except that it doesn't always show up at the right time. I was supposed to be correcting a book that had been advertised everywhere. An anxious publisher was waiting for it. That's not the time to let yourself get distracted by something new. But a good subject sets off energy in me that's like physical passion. It's all I could think about.

*Brussels Hotel*

By the time I left Tallahassee, I had surrendered to the monster. I got to the Brussels Book Fair. What a reception! They welcomed me with such ceremony—but it was Haiti they were taking into their hearts. I had interviews everywhere. Belgian intellectuals (Yvon Toussaint, Jean-Luc Outers) were deeply moved by the Haitian tragedy. I saw the same thing in the schools. I'd never witnessed such fervor toward a nation. The grade-school students who went to the fair with their teachers asked me about the history of the country instead of just the recent events. They were interested in daily life there. The questions were well thought out and most of them touched on love and death. They had all read *Je suis fou de Vava* and *La fête des morts*. Eyes open wide, they asked all kinds of hard and essential questions. Do you still love Vava? Can you love the same person your whole life through? Do people die differently in Haiti? Can you love someone even after death? Whose death: yours or the other person's? Laughter. A short interlude when I didn't think of my book. Then I ran back to the hotel room. Frenzy: I was writing non-stop. If that kept up, with no writer's block, I'd finish the earthquake book in five days, and use the remaining six to correct *Notes*. The room was well lit. Through the window, I could see the trees gently stirring. Anything that moves still scared me. I dove back into the book. That feeling of reliving everything, moment by moment. I had to make choices to keep from getting lost in the details. I was writing this book as much for myself as for others. Everyone who hadn't been there. A friend, Ann Gerrard, protected me by telling everyone that I wasn't available, without giving any explanations. I met up with Alain Mabanckou at the "Échappées africaines" booth. He was in a hurry too. We took a little time to talk. He had been expected in Port-au-Prince on January 13. When the earthquake struck, he was finishing a book illuminated by the presence of his mother: the Pauline Kengué I wrote about in *The Return*. In that book, Pauline dies in Haiti. Of her, I wrote, "She always said she'd come here so Alain would feel Haitian when the time came." I felt that fate was awaiting him in Port-au-Prince. Good thing he didn't make it. He was the first to announce that I was still alive. Our constant correspondence keeps us friends. I woke up early to write, then packed my bag and took a taxi for the station.

## The Train

The ride from Brussels to Paris lasts a little over an hour. I decided to use the time to empty out my mind. Rest my spirit. Watch the undulations of the landscape. These lands haven't known hurricanes or earthquakes for quite a while (but two world wars will do). Nature seems solid here. But I know that all Atlas has to do is shrug his shoulders and everything will tip into horror. I didn't want those violent images. Can't I have peace and quiet any more? Extreme fatigue is pushing me into a tunnel of darkness. But I know how to find peace. From deep in childhood, I conjure up my grandmother's smiling face. Sleep follows. The next thing I know, the train is pulling into the station.

## Paris Hotel

I want nothing else but this little book about the earthquake I'm writing. It isn't long, but it has captured me by stirring up dark emotions I thought were well hidden in my memory. I'm not the kind who cries in public. Big events never make me cry. I get teary-eyed over silly things, like a flower losing its petals in the wind. I went to my favorite district in Paris where there are plenty of bookstores. To my eyes, Paris is the most beautiful city in the world. But it's a hard place. Don't try being poor in Paris. I went to that little hotel that dates back to 1890. Everything dates back to another century in Paris. Nothing moves here. It's the opposite of Port-au-Prince, where everything is moving. Now I have to tell my publisher that he won't be getting the book he's expecting, but another one. Meanwhile, he's been talking up the first one for the last month. He'll have to get word out to his network. He knows I'm unpredictable, but reliable. He'll always get a book, even if it's not the one he was expecting. One book was hiding behind the first. A month ago, I was saying No to publishers who wanted me to write about the earthquake. And it's still No. I was working on the notes I took in Port-au-Prince while the events were still fresh in my mind and my body. That's not what I call a book. It was my private life put into words. I agreed to open up a little about what happened so that other people wouldn't feel alone with their emotions. Now I have to face the music. My publisher is waiting. He's in a state. He's pacing the room, phone jammed against his ear. He's playing publisher, the way that I'm playing writer. We both have cracks in our structures, and we don't know when the cracks will bring down the whole construction. So we have to act fast. The machine can break down at any time. And I say that without pathos. Just as well, since this is a book that could be written only in a state of emergency. At the hotel, I go downstairs and tell the guy at the desk that I don't need my room cleaned for the next few days. A surprised look. I end up explaining that I'm finishing a book that I have to give my publisher in the very near future. The guy smiles broadly. One of the few cities in the world where the writer is sacred. They start sending tea to my room. They even offer to filter my phone calls. "Give me the names, sir, of the two or three people you wish to speak to. For the others, I'll take a message." I write with a cup of tea. The way Oscar Wilde did on his last trip to Paris. He stayed in his room, reading Balzac and drinking tea. The only luxury that counted for him was being in Paris. I get up early and write. As long as I'm writing, nothing moves. Writing keeps things from breaking down. But you can't spend your life writing, knowing that everything will collapse as soon as you stop. You'd like to stay in this dream world. Alice will go back through the looking glass. In reality, people don't live in hotels in Paris or anywhere else; they sleep in tents. They have to fight for something to eat, and they watch the sky with apprehension. Although that's no reason to sleep under a bridge. There's no sense imitating other people's poverty. It's better to act so that one day they will sleep in clean sheets and spend their days in idle thoughts that sweeten life. This is the last day. In the room next to mine, a couple is making love. On that music, I will finish the book.

DANY LAFFERIÈRE was born in Port-au-Prince, Haiti, in 1953. He is the author of fourteen novels, including *I Am a Japanese Writer*, *Heading South*, and the award-winning *How to Make Love to a Negro without Getting Tired*. Laferrière is the recipient of numerous literary awards, including the Prix Carbet des Lycéens, the Prix Médicis, and the Governor General's Literary Award. He lives in Montreal.

DAVID HOMEL, born and raised in Chicago, is a Governor General Literary Award-winning translator and writer who lives in Montreal. His recent books include the translations of *The Last Genet: A Writer in Revolt* and *The Inverted Gaze* (both Arsenal Pulp) and his own novel *Midway* (Cormorant).